WISDOM'S
FRIENDS

Other books by Sharon H. Ringe
from Westminster John Knox Press

Luke (Westminster Bible Companion)
Women's Bible Commentary, Expanded Edition
(Coeditor, with Carol A. Newsom)

WISDOM'S FRIENDS

COMMUNITY AND CHRISTOLOGY IN THE FOURTH GOSPEL

Sharon H. Ringe

Westminster John Knox Press
Louisville, Kentucky

Book design by Sharon Adams

First edition
Published by Westminster John Knox Press
Louisville, Kentucky

This book is printed on acid-free paper that meets the American National Standards Institute Z39.48 standard. ♾

PRINTED IN THE UNITED STATES OF AMERICA

99 00 01 02 03 04 05 06 07 08 — 10 9 8 7 6 5 4 3 2 1

Library of Congress Cataloging-in-Publication Data

A catalog record for this book is available from the Library of Congress.

ISBN 0-664-25714-3

To faculty colleagues and friends at
Wesley Theological Seminary,
Universidad Bíblica Latinoamericana,
and
Methodist Theological School in Ohio,
with thanks, respect, and affection!

Contents

Preface

Every book has a biography—a story of its life. Key events establish its genre, scope, and depth, and the interaction between book and author establishes its shape and contours. This work had, in retrospect, three catalytic moments that, in the beginning, gave no hint of the project in which they would come to life. The first came in my study, in preparation for a class in which I was trying to unsnarl the dynamics of Paul's relationship with Christians at Galatia. The tighter the snarl seemed to get, the deeper I probed. Prompted by the commentary on that letter by Hans Dieter Betz,[1] I began to study what Hellenistic philosophers had to say about friendship. While I was not persuaded that this had a lot to do with Paul and Galatia, I kept saying to myself, "But this sounds like the Gospel of John!" Thus began step one of the study.

The second event took place over an extended period of time. I spend part of almost every summer teaching at el Seminario Bíblico Latinoamericano (now la Universidad Bíblica Latinoamericana) in San José, Costa Rica. Our students there come from all over Central America and from many countries of South America and the Caribbean. Many come with the experience of years of work in various movements of liberation, and in church communities decimated by the various countries' death squads. These students speak about their ministry as *una pastoral de acompañamiento*—a ministry of accompaniment—in which their principal responsibility is solidarity with entire communities under siege, or with those in other communities who are under threat from the conditions of war in which they live, or who are suffering from economic hardship, or racist, sexist, or other forms of exploitation. Their ministry involves identifying with these groups, sharing their fate if necessary, and refusing to be dislodged even when their own lives are on the line. I will never forget the first time I was assigned to teach in the classroom named for

Noel Vargas. Not a major donor, such as North Americans might choose for naming classrooms and other spaces, Noel was a Baptist pastor from Nicaragua, a graduate of the seminary, who was tortured to death by the Contras. I challenge you to try to teach theology in front of his portrait! Try looking into the eyes of students whom you might be preparing for a similar witness! This sounds, I said to myself, a lot like the "friendship" of John's Gospel, but even more like the vision of the church centered on the "other Paraclete (or Advocate)" whose advent is promised to accompany the church as its life unfolds.

The third "aha!," chronologically speaking, came as the political and theological furor in many Protestant denominations over the "Re-imagining Conference," which was organized in conjunction with the Ecumenical Decade of the Churches in Solidarity with Women (1988–98),[2] pushed me into work on texts in the Hebrew Bible and the deuterocanonical literature that develop the theme of Wisdom, or Sophia. This work again led me back to the Fourth Gospel, and quickly beyond the trite observation that the hymn with which that Gospel begins sounds like a hymn to Sophia, sung now in a different key. The more I immersed myself in Sophia traditions, the more clearly I came to recognize them in the richly textured christological language of this Gospel—not as the author's only christological category, but certainly among those by which that author tried to point toward the reality and the power of Jesus for the community to which the Gospel was addressed.

These three starting points came together into this project when I recognized that all three converged in the identity and vocation of both the community out of which this Gospel emerged and to which it was addressed, and in the identity and vocation of the Christ at its center. The specific intertwining of these investigations into the Fourth Gospel became the occasion of a kind of case study in Christology and ecclesiology as two sides of a single theological agenda. That set of concerns has a theoretical component, seen in the integrity of images, concepts, and literary forms by which the Gospel unfolds. There is a component of praxis as well, which comes to expression in the integrity of the Gospel with the community's historical and social context, and in the continuing challenge of the Gospel to the life of contemporary churches.

The linear structure required by a book conflicts with both the evolution and the content of this project. Both form webs of cross-references and flashbacks, images that spin themselves out and then transform themselves in unexpected directions. Were the project being done a few years later, I would probably abandon the printed medium in favor of a more textured and flexible hypertext format. Lacking the technical skills to produce such a creature, I have pulled apart the interconnections for the purpose of examination and study. I hope, however, that the result leaves their deeper links still intact.

The double pairs of content (christological confession and Christian community) and commitment (critical theological reflection and the practice of ministry) that are embodied in this study mirror my own identity. I come to this study as a New Testament scholar and seminary professor on the one hand, and as an ordained minister in the United Church of Christ and (as one friend described me) a "chronic missionary" on the other. My academic work cannot be conducted in isolation from my commitment to the embodiment of the gospel in the communities and institutions of our contemporary world, and my work of ministry requires that I bring to the communities where I serve the challenge of critical reflection on the roots and consequences of our faith.

Appropriately, this study evolved in the twin contexts of the academy—study, classroom, and lecture hall—and church study groups. Many seminary students and lay people have helped to shape and to clarify my work by their questions and suggestions, and I am grateful to all of them. Adult Sunday School classes at Rockville United Church, Georgetown Presbyterian Church, and Luther Place Church (all in the Washington, D.C., area) have joined students at Wesley Theological Seminary in keeping the various steps of this study firmly grounded. I appreciate the opportunities provided by Bangor Theological Seminary in Bangor, Maine (through the 1996 Francis B. Denio Lectures on the Bible) and United Theological Seminary in Dayton, Ohio (through the 1997 J. Balmer Showers Lectures), for the stimulus to pull together portions of this research, and for the stimulation to further work that was provided by the ensuing discussions.

My heartfelt thanks go to the Board of Governors and the Administration of Wesley Theological Seminary for funding the sabbatical leave that allowed me to bring this project to completion. I am grateful to faculty colleagues, and especially to my colleagues in the biblical field, who took on the extra work that made my absence possible. I would also like to thank Roger Butts for his help with the Index and Carey Newman and his colleagues on the editorial staff of Westminster John Knox Press, who provided the wise guidance and the friendly support that enabled hunches to become words, as I struggled to understand the Word-become-flesh and the model Friend of this Gospel.

This study has taught me a lot about Wisdom and about friendship, but I really came to know both through the wise friends and friends of Wisdom with whom it has been my privilege to teach over the past two decades. It is to these colleagues at Wesley Theological Seminary, la Universidad Bíblica Latinoamericana, and the Methodist Theological School in Ohio that this book is dedicated.

Abbreviations

AB	Anchor Bible
BAGD	W. Bauer, W. F. Arndt, F. W. Gingrich, and F. W. Danker, *Greek-English Lexicon of the New Testament*
BDB	F. Brown, S. R. Driver, and C. A. Briggs, *Hebrew and English Lexicon of the Old Testament*
BJS	Brown Judaic Studies
CBQ	*Catholic Biblical Quarterly*
HSM	Harvard Semitic Monographs
Int	*Interpretation*
JBL	*Journal of Biblical Literature*
JSNT	*Journal for the Study of the New Testament*
JSNTSup	*Journal for the Study of the New Testament* Supplement Series
JSOT	*Journal for the Study of the Old Testament*
JSOTSup	*Journal for the Study of the Old Testament* Supplement Series
NIB	New Interpreter's Bible
NovT	*Novum Testamentum*
NovTSup	Supplements to *Novum Testamentum*
OBT	Overtures to Biblical Theology
OTL	Old Testament Library
SBL	Society of Biblical Literature
SBLDS	SBL Dissertation Series
SBLMS	SBL Monograph Series
SBLRBS	SBL Resources for Biblical Study
SJLA	Studies in Judaism in Late Antiquity
SNTSMS	Society of New Testament Studies Monograph Series
TDNT	G. Kittel and G. Friedrich (eds.), *Theological Dictionary of the New Testament* (10 vols.)
UBSGNT	United Bible Societies' edition of the Greek New Testament
VT	*Vetus Testamentum*

Chapter 1

Wisdom and Friendship: Images of Christ and Church

"In the beginning was the Word, and the Word was with God, and the Word was God." The words are familiar. If we are Christians, we hear them—capital letters and all—as the first line of a poem whose rhythmic cadences and repetitious words affirm the preexistence of Jesus Christ proclaimed in the Gospel that follows. That Gospel struggles to hold on to its unique voice against the background of the close harmony of the Synoptic Gospels (Matthew, Mark, and Luke), which themselves lose their individual accents as they are blended into a single melody that defines Jesus for believers.

This study takes a closer look at that familiar poetry as an expression of divine Wisdom, whose story is celebrated in the Hebrew Bible and the deuterocanonical literature. That background celebrates Wisdom's intimacy with God and her role in the creation, and it identifies other motifs of her subsequent vocation to search for a people who will feast at her banquet and follow the "way" she teaches and thus become "friends of God" (Wisd. Sol. 7:27). The traditions about divine Wisdom, in turn, highlight specific accents in the remainder of the Fourth Gospel that affirm the Gospel writer's understanding both of Jesus as the Christ and of the community called into being around him. They are called "friends" by the one who embodied God's own love among them and showed them the way of friendship (John 15:12–17).

Divine Wisdom: co-creator with God of all that is and simply a friend, someone bound to us neither by blood nor by law or church sacrament—someone of whom we would say, "She's just a friend." The evangelical hymn proclaims, "What a friend we have in Jesus," in a picture of intimacy and tenderness that is the polar opposite of the majesty of the one who was with God "in the beginning," "light of all people," "full of grace and truth" (John 1:2, 4, 14). Yet both affirmations are confessed to be true, and, according to the Fourth Gospel, both shape the identity of Jesus and of the community alike. As hard as it may be for linear logic to hold those two poles together, the power of poetry and of the narrative imagery of the Gospel succeed precisely in linking the lofty celebration of the first with the feet-on-the-ground faithfulness of the second. The paradox they embody illustrates with crystal clarity the truth recognized by Diego Irarrázaval: "Christian theology is not a mental and doctrinal labor. Rather, it is a loving relationship with God that leads to celebration, transformation, knowledge. It is, as Jon Sobrino puts it, an *intellectus amoris*."[1]

WISDOM AND FRIENDSHIP—CHRIST
AND COMMUNITY INTERTWINED

A meditation on John 1:1–18 from the Iona community in Scotland joins the majesty of wisdom and the intimacy of friendship in the resulting hymn-text:

> Before the world began, one Word was there;
> Grounded in God he was, rooted in care;
> By him all things were made, in him was love displayed;
> Through him God spoke, and said, "I AM FOR YOU."
>
> Life found in him its source, death found its end;
> Light found in him its course, darkness its friend.
> For neither death nor doubt nor darkness can put out
> The glow of God, the shout, "I AM FOR YOU."
>
> The Word was in the world which from him came;
> Unrecognized he was, unknown by name;
> One with all humankind, with the unloved aligned,
> Convincing sight and mind, "I AM FOR YOU."
>
> All who received the Word by God were blessed;
> Sisters and brothers they of earth's fond guest.
> So did the Word of Grace proclaim in time and space
> And with a human face, "I AM FOR YOU."[2]

John 1:1–18 accentuates the majestic side of the paradox, with mere hints of the consequences that ensue when the Word becomes flesh (John 1:14). The paradox that is held together so tightly in the modern hymn is completed in the Gospel narrative, which portrays Jesus' engagement and solidarity with humankind that mirror the vocation and quest of divine Wisdom for acceptance and for a people who receive her and, in that receiving, are transformed. Just as her presence assures order in the world and in human life where she is received, so Jesus also embodies the coherence of time and space, of the social order, and of life itself for the Johannine community in its liminal situation in the Jewish Diaspora, and again on the edges of the synagogue community.[3] He assures them of—even embodies— God's presence with them in concrete and ordinary moments of their life as a community, as they live as friends of one another.

The picture of Jesus as at once Wisdom incarnate and the Friend who befriends others and commands them to be friends to one another is developed through a wealth of images and narrative instances. These images and narratives make their appeal to the readers of the Fourth Gospel, not through rational argument, but rather in "expressive thought" that addresses the emotions and the imagination. This performative language also builds a community, as a people coalesces that claims and is claimed by it.[4] That community, in turn, becomes the way that God's love for the world—which was seen in the passion of the creation and in Wisdom's longing for a home on earth, and which was incarnate in Jesus—continues to be embodied in the creation.

In the dominant culture of North America, at least in the modern age, the category of friendship risks trivialization and sentimentalization.[5] In the popular perception, friends fall into a chasm between calls for a return to "family values" and the quest to network and make business-related "contacts." While changing demographics find many people living far away from members of their families of origin (and living longer following the death of a spouse or other life's companion), changing patterns of adult relationships and "family" constellations find many turning again to "friend" as a category of intimacy and reliability that makes life possible and even pleasurable in the modern world. The hymn referred to earlier, "What a Friend We Have in Jesus," is near the top of the list of requests by elderly residents of nursing homes who are all too aware of the loss of those human friends, as well as family members, who had blessed their lives in their younger, "better" days.

With that renewed recognition of what many ancient philosophers recognized about the value of friendship in human life, friendship has found its way into theological discourse as well in these closing decades of the twentieth century. Mary Hunt has claimed the tender strength of women's friendship as a fresh lens for refocusing the entire task of theological reflection.[6] Friendship is one of the "models of God" developed by Sallie McFague,[7] as she identifies "sustaining" as the paradigmatic activity of God as friend and "companionship" as the hallmark of divine ethics. Two studies explicitly link the theme of friendship to the Fourth Gospel. Josephine Massyngbaerde Ford explores implications for Johannine Christology, while Eldo Puthenkandathil examines "friend" as a title of discipleship.[8] In his comprehensive study of the church in the New Testament, Jürgen Roloff points to the prominence of friendship in the Fourth Gospel to emphasize that "what passes for the church" in the Fourth Gospel is really Christ's community with individual believers, and the church is appropriately identified as "the community of the friends of Jesus."[9] Jürgen Moltmann tempers the individualism of Roloff to speak of the church as "the community of friends." That friendship, he maintains, has a christological focus, in that it is Jesus' "death in friendship" that makes the disciples his friends forever. Furthermore, through the commandment that they also are to love one another, "open friendship" becomes the bond and vocation defining their community with one another.[10]

Wisdom, like friendship, also must be recognized in narrative images present in the Fourth Gospel that relate both to the meaning of Jesus as the Christ—Christology—and to the definition of community—ecclesiology. Wisdom who teaches God's way and hosts a generous banquet (see, for example, Prov. 9:5–6) is defeated unless she finds people who accept her, and one cannot be a friend alone. For the Fourth Gospel, then, one way of speaking of "the church" is as the community called into being around Wisdom, which is also the community defined by the gift and demand of friendship with God, Christ, and one another. The question of the identity of Christians is thus related to the identity of Jesus.[11] Jesus as the λόγος who became flesh both maintains the relationship between the believers, God, and each other and defines the community as those who keep that same λόγος in the form of the commandment to love one another (John 15:12–17).

Paul Minear argues that the Logos—meaning both the λόγος of John 1:1–18 and the word of teaching or commandment—must be seen as primarily a category of ecclesiology that also conditions the meaning of Christ in the Fourth Gospel.[12] That same "logos-symbol," he maintains, links the prologue (1:1–18) to the rest of the Gospel by its connection to the words and speech of Jesus and thus discloses the interdependence of ecclesiology and Christology by referring both to Jesus and to that which convokes the community. It was necessary to the theological project of the Fourth Gospel that "the logos the evangelist discovered at work in the church of his day be traced to the glory of God before the foundation of the world."[13] At the same time, that community itself owes its very existence to the presence of the λόγος: "Ultimately it is God's logos that creates the community of God's children and abides within that community."[14] That symbol indicates not only the cohesive element in the existing community but also the fabric that connects that community to its ancestors and its descendants, linking the present life of the church to its primal origins.

Minear's emphasis on ecclesiology as the principal category for interpreting the Johannine λόγος puts a fresh spin on the question of whether there even is an ecclesiology in the Fourth Gospel. Johan Ferreira summarizes the state of scholarship on that question,[15] concluding that there is general agreement that the Fourth Gospel has a definite ecclesiology that is closely related to its Christology, even though there is no evident system of sacraments or of church offices. Rather, the church is the community of those gathered by the ones Jesus sent, and, in fact, it is more appropriate to talk about "community" than church in relationship to the Fourth Gospel. The basis of that community is the revelation it has from Jesus, and the character or inner life of the community is the joy it has in the Word, in the unity that is its gift from Christ (John 17), and in the members' love for one another. Its purpose is to carry forward the original sending of the Son into the world. Ferreira's christological focus in the discussion of the church in the Fourth Gospel develops suggestions already put forward in Ernst Käsemann's study of the prayer of John 17 (with its obvious focus on the approaching death of Jesus) as the principal lens into the author's view of the essential unity of the church in Christ—a unity which is also the community's vocation.[16] Rudolf Schnackenburg also concludes that Christology is the focal interest of the Fourth Gospel and its understanding of the community gathered around that center. The absence of the word ἐκκλησία or any reference to offices or issues of church order, coupled with the apparent competition between Peter and "the disciple whom Jesus loved" (seen in John 20:1–10, for example), however, leads him to conclude that the Johannine community is sectarian, and not a central part of the early church.[17] Wes Howard-Brook emphasizes the radical difference between the view of the church in this Gospel (as "an egalitarian community led by the elusive presence of the *paraclete*" or Spirit of truth [John 14:16–17; 15:26]—a tight gathering of persons with Jesus at the center) and the emerging institution that can be found elsewhere in the New

Testament.[18] On the other hand, he observes that the heart of the Gospel narrative that takes the story from the Feast of Tabernacles in John 7:1–8:59 to the Passion itself shows that the "high" Christology of this Gospel "is not proclaimed for its own sake, but for its power to generate and sustain a community of discipleship."[19] That community with the vocation to carry forward the healing and redemptive work of the Sent One who has called it into being is precisely what the Fourth Gospel means by the church.

In other words, at the heart of the picture of the church in the Fourth Gospel is a model of accompaniment that is seen paradigmatically in Jesus' life as it embodies dimensions of Wisdom and friendship. The same model is carried on in the church through the "other Paraclete," the Spirit of truth (14:16), who "becomes flesh" in the community of believers. Friendship and Wisdom are thus related as much to ecclesiology as to Christology—or perhaps for the author of the Fourth Gospel they are ecclesiological precisely because they are christological. The gift of Christ as Wisdom/ὁ λόγος was to seek out a community to instruct in God's way, to sustain with the bread and water of life, and also to befriend and make into friends of one another. The demand of the church is that its members be friends in this serious way, so that the narrative of divine presence in human flesh can go on. Comforting in time of hardship, standing together in the face of danger, caring when someone is sick, even "laying down" one's life for a friend, and in all of this remaining united with Christ, with God, and with one another—these images of friendship lend specific content and consequences to the "other" who re-presents in the church the λόγος who became flesh, the one sent from God, whom the Fourth Gospel calls Way, Truth, and Life.

PRESUPPOSITIONS ABOUT CHRISTOLOGY AND ECCLESIOLOGY

Four presuppositions about Christology and ecclesiology undergird this study. Those presuppositions are that, for any given author or other interpreter, the meaning of the Christ and the view of the community called in Christ's name are (1) interdependent, (2) expressed through metaphors, (3) plural rather than unitary, and (4) closely linked to the interpreter's context. These assumptions are so fundamental to this study that, while they may be self-evident, each merits a brief explanatory discussion.

Interdependent

Christology and ecclesiology are like two sides of a single coin. Neither has consistent temporal priority. Rather, as one comes into being, so does the other. As soon as a person or a community begins to discuss the meaning of Christ, they have already implied key qualities of the community drawn together in Christ's name. Likewise, as soon as they have identified the marks of the church, they have begun to sketch the contours of the Christ in whom the church has its being. Neither Christology nor ecclesiology is consistently the cause, while the other is the consequence. In fact, they are not sequentially or even systematically related, such that a doctrine of Christ can be developed, and then an appropriate view of the church can be derived from it (or, conversely, that a particular view of the church gives birth to talk about Christ that conforms to it). Rather, what is said about Christ already carries with it an understanding of church, and the life of a church already sets the framework giving shape to the Christ who is confessed. There is no point in arguing whether the christological chicken preceded the ecclesiological egg! The Christology and ecclesiology of any community, including that of the Fourth Gospel, are of a piece.[20]

Metaphorical

The second presupposition undergirding this study is that Christology and ecclesiology are inherently metaphorical. I use that term in its popular, generic sense to encompass all types of imagistic speech that point toward an "object" without claiming to name it directly. Sallie McFague has already established that the only way to speak of a truly transcendent God using finite speech is with metaphors or, more properly, "models" that include a more complex web of consequent relationships and entanglements.[21] Elisabeth Schüssler Fiorenza likewise affirms, "G*d-language is symbolic, metaphoric, and analogous because human language can never speak adequately about divine reality."[22] The problem of finding adequate ways to speak about God increases geometrically when one tries to speak about Christ and about the community convened by and "in" Christ, because one is speaking at once about transcendent reality and human specificity. The problem is like trying to speak two languages at once!

In this study I use "image" as the encompassing term for metaphorical language that both shapes and reflects reality and thus expresses the world in which one's action takes place. The limits of the range of images at one's disposal set the limits of the world one can envision. One's system of images is rooted in particular social, cultural, political, economic contexts, such that the most powerful images come from one's own culture and secondarily from transcultural exploration. Images are "interested," in that they embody a value system. Since they form as well as reflect the context of one's life, they have the power to change one's world and reorient one's life. Images accomplish such orientation by combining familiar terms and perspectives in new ways that challenge predictability and inertia. Their juxtaposition of familiar and strange elements provokes initial cracks in one's preconceptions, which make clear the limiting political consequences of one's prior vision of the world and move one toward action and transformation. Images are tensive and elastic, acquiring new accents and elaborations as they are reused in new situations. Images perform an integrative function, bridging separate fields of inquiry and arenas of life, and thus are particularly well suited to express such interdependent arenas of discourse as Christology and ecclesiology. Images engage the imagination and evoke responses, like the beads and shards of glass sealed in a kaleidoscope that form new designs at the slightest touch. To interpret an image or plumb its meanings includes investigating the historically and culturally relative moments of its origin and subsequent use, as well as recognizing the new meanings that occur in its interaction with the contemporary interpreter. In this way one avoids universalizing meanings from another time and place and canon- izing them as the only legitimate interpretation.[23]

A community's language about Christ provides a normative statement of its view of the meaning of the gospel for the world. Christological images establish the contours of the world in which action takes place, and thus they also set the contours of the perception of the community linked to Christ by faith and practice. The result is a set of stylized pictures intended to convey meaning, not to report information. To speak of Christ imagistically or parabolically is to speak theo- centrically, not christocentrically, since to speak of Christ is to speak of one who is transparent to God. The Fourth Gospel escalates that affirmation to say that Christ *is* God, and thus it makes clear the fact that we can no more speak literally about Christ, or about the community gathered in Christ's name, than we can speak literally about God. Any statements about Christ are thus prototypes—first state- ments begging to be reformed, re-imaged, and transformed as they intersect our lives, and as we glimpse anew God's nature, presence, and will.

Plural

The third presupposition about Christology and ecclesiology that undergirds this study is that both are plural. The study does not claim that the intertwining of Wisdom and friendship defines *the* Johannine Christology and ecclesiology. Rather, it claims that Wisdom and friendship together form one crucial thread in a complex textual tapestry. The usual way the question is framed about the rich variety of christological motifs and titles in the Fourth Gospel is whether that va- riety reflects different sources or stages in the Gospel's development. I would re- spond instead that such variety is intrinsic to christological reflection, and thus a necessary factor in the work of the evangelist. For this reason, while I am intrigued by the intention of Paul N. Anderson to focus a study of the "unity and disunity" of Johannine Christology through the lens of John 6, the unitary project betrayed in the title of his book (*The Christology of the Fourth Gospel*) is problematical. Similarly, the effort of Robert Gordon Maccini to analyze the Fourth Gospel's por- trayal of Jesus and of the Johannine community under the single rubric of legal language and narratives (such as the terms "testimony," "testify," "command- ments," and "judgments," and the call and witness pattern of such pericopes as 1:43–51; 4:7–42; and chapter 11)[24] risks flattening the multidimensional project that the Fourth Gospel presents.

The author of the Fourth Gospel appears to recognize the necessity for a plu- rality of designations of Jesus' nature and authority in the avalanche of titles and functions by which Jesus is introduced in John 1:19–51. He is the one who stands among you, whom you do not know; one coming after John; one whose sandals John is not worthy to untie; the Lamb of God who takes away the sin of the world; one who ranks ahead of John and existed before him; one on whom the Spirit de- scends and remains; one who baptizes with the Holy Spirit; Child of God; Rabbi— and the list goes on. That list itself proves inadequate, as the Gospel unfolds with story after story—"sign" after sign—that define this One who remains with them, befriending them and making them into friends.

While it is not possible to compile a similar list of ways the Fourth Gospel identifies the community around Jesus and the subsequent church, both what is and what is not said about them point in a parallel direction of diversity. Jesus' followers are called simply "the disciples," "friends" (15:12–17), and "those whom you gave me" (17:6). The later communities, including that from which the Fourth Gospel emerged, share those identities and, in addition, are called "those who will believe in me through their [Jesus' immediate followers'] word" (17:20). Missing are formal titles of authority—even ἀπόστολος, though Jesus and his followers are all said to have been "sent"—and designations of the church (such as the term ἐκκλησία) that suggest the movement toward increased institutionalization and uniformity that one sees in such literature as the pastoral epistles, which are roughly contemporary to the Fourth Gospel. There, language and reflection that had its roots in a plurality of voices and in imagistic speech give way to univocal, rational argument and to universal truth claims.

Contextual

Given the power of a community's confession about the Christ and of the shape and life of the community itself, christological and ecclesiological images are especially difficult to rescue from this magnetic attraction toward claims of universal and univocal meaning. It is important to recognize, however, that the historical traditions and cultural matrices of each confessing community influence the pool of images available for its christological and ecclesiological reflection. The economic, social, and political systems that are taken for granted in the surrounding society; assumptions about how the non-human natural world functions; the ideologies related to gender, social and economic class, ethnicity, and religion that shape the data of existence into meaningful constructs; and the pastoral needs, crises, hopes, and longings of the community inevitably privilege some images and exclude others. As circumstances change or new believers from different contexts enter the community, some of the previously viable images may come to seem unrelated or even contradictory to the new reality. These images then fall into disuse, and new ones take shape. At the outset of any study of Christology and ecclesiology, therefore, it is essential to be aware of the specific circumstances and identity of the community from which those affirmations and practices arose.

STRUCTURE OF THIS STUDY

Given the importance of context in shaping Christology and ecclesiology, this study must begin with an analysis of the circumstances of the Johannine community as a subgroup defined by its christological allegiance to Jesus, living in the final decade and a half of the first century in a community of the Jewish Diaspora (chapter 2). Against the backdrop of that attempt to understand the historical, cultural, and religious dynamics facing such a community, we then explore the understanding of Wisdom that the Johannine community would have inherited in the traditions concerning divine Wisdom in the Hebrew Bible and deuterocanonical books (chapter 3). Chapter 4 examines how those traditions unfold in the Fourth Gospel, beginning with the hymn of John 1:1–18 and its echoes through the rest of the Gospel, and then looks at other motifs associated with divine Wisdom that are attributed to Jesus and to the community convened around him by the Gospel traditions received and shaped by the Johannine community. Chapter 5 carries out a similar examination of motifs of friendship in the Christology and ecclesiology of the Fourth Gospel, as these are carried in specific vocabulary, in John 15:12–17 (the central passage on friendship), and through other attributes of friendship that echo the reflections on friendship among Hellenistic philosophers and in the biblical narratives about David and Jonathan (in 2 Samuel) and Ruth and Naomi (in the book of Ruth). The figure of the Paraclete (examined in chapter 6) is crucial to seeing how the Johannine community conceived of the continuing presence of Christ as Wisdom /ὁ λόγος, even though that one has returned "above" to dwell no longer on earth, but with God. The conclusion (chapter 7) draws together the results of this study and explores implications for the life of the contemporary church and the field of New Testament theology.

Chapter 2

Getting to Know the Johannine Community

The metaphors and rhetoric by which the Fourth Gospel speaks of Christ and the church stretch the modern reader's imagination. We are tempted to allow our minds and hearts to color the words with the palette of our own spirituality and to adorn them with the decorations supplied by centuries of church doctrine. The task of interpretation requires attention to the meanings evoked in such responses, but also to the question of what was accomplished in the lives of the original audience through their encounter with the text, and how the specific terms of this Gospel would have touched their pastoral and theological concerns. An important aspect of that inquiry is thus getting to know the community that gave rise to the Fourth Gospel. Unfortunately, there is no clear external evidence to the location, composition, or circumstances of the community. Such details are discerned between the lines and underneath the language of the Gospel itself by carefully combing the text for clues to the composition and experience of the community, then reweaving those threads into a fabric that approaches as closely as possible the original design.

This task of reweaving, or of historical reconstruction, is not peculiar to this Gospel, but rather is essential to the reading of any Gospel. This is the case because, while the Gospel writer's focus is on Jesus' life and ministry, the point of that story is not a neutral report or the product of the individual creativity of the author, but rather a demonstration of the significance of Jesus for the life of the community from and to which the Gospel was written.[1] The author works from a stereoptic gaze that pays attention to the traditions about Jesus that the community has inherited and, at the same time, to the pastoral needs for which those traditions are being recast. Both the cultural and religious assumptions of the community and the specific factors of its social composition and immediate historical experience have shaped those questions and concerns that Jesus and the Gospel were seen to address. The question of the community of origin looms especially large in the case of the Fourth Gospel, because it is at once so markedly different from the three Synoptic Gospels in the shape of the narrative and in its constituent details, and yet it claims the same Jesus of Nazareth as its foundation. How can we account for the commonalities, and what forces appear to have shaped the differences?

At issue is the community in its specificity. Categories traditionally used to classify the origins or roots of this Gospel—"Jewish" or "Greek," churchly or sectarian—prove unhelpful, largely because of their inherent ambiguity in the first-century Hellenistic world (itself a single term that masks the variety of combinations of social, cultural, economic, political, and religious influences to be found in it).[2] This reconstruction of the Johannine community replaces general claims about "Jewish Christianity" or about such larger historical movements as the evolving relationship between "church" and "synagogue" or between "Christianity" and "Judaism" with a more deeply textured picture reconstructed from the Gospel writer's own clues about this individual community of believers and its relationship to its community of origin.

The clues on which we draw are found in the overall narrative design of the story, the language by which it is told (both specific terms and their syntactical framework), the narratives and teachings included in it, the characters who populate it, the cultural practices it assumes, the places to which it refers, asides from the narrator to the implied audience, and other devices. At issue is not whether the author intended to offer such clues, for what an author intended beyond what that author wrote can never be known. Instead, the question is what the presence of such clues indicates about the people to whom the work was directed, and with whom the author apparently hoped to communicate the significance of Jesus.

Like most interpreters of the final decades of the twentieth century, I assume that the author of this Gospel was not an eyewitness reporting events of Jesus' life. Instead, I conclude that the author drew on a variety of traditions filtered through several decades of the community's life and reflection, and wrote this work sometime in the final two decades of the first century.[3] Undoubtedly those traditions included a fairly complete narrative of the passion and death of Jesus, much of the material presented as the farewell discourse of chapters 13–17, and collections of stories of Jesus' public ministry (on the order of, but not necessarily identical to, what has been called the "signs source"[4]). The core of this material is attributed to the anonymous "disciple whom Jesus loved," but it is likely that before the author began to work with it, that core material already bore the stamp of the intervening life of the community. That the Gospel tells the church's story along with Jesus' story can be seen in the first-person plural pronouns attributed to Jesus to refer to his work (3:11; 9:4): What Jesus has done is what "we" continue to do.

The author is concerned with issues of the late first century, such as the relationship between this community and other Christian communities, notably those centered around the leadership of Peter. This "ecumenical" agenda can be recognized in Peter's reintroduction for the commission to carry on the task of the "good shepherd" in chapter 21, after a relatively minor role (certainly compared to the Synoptic Gospels and Acts) in the earlier part of the Gospel. Clearly the question of the relationship between John's community and the Jews around it has reached crisis proportions, at least in the author's perception. Perhaps as a consequence of these various external stresses, the author also has to address internal questions of unity and lifestyle within the community (John 15–17). Parallels are drawn between the way Jesus is portrayed in the community gathered around him and the way Jesus continues to be known—at least according to the author—in the Johannine community as it wrestles with these and other issues in its context.

Factors such as these work together to define the context within which the basic belief structure and theology of the community are forged. Elements of that context that require elaboration are the language in which the Gospel is written, the location and social composition of the community, the role of "the Jews," and the relationship between this community and other Christian groups of the late first century. Against the background of these discussions, it will be possible to sketch the contours of the "Johannine community"—that is, the community to which the Fourth Gospel was addressed, and whose history and experiences shaped the traditions about Jesus that it had received.

LANGUAGE

A good place to begin the reconstruction of the picture of the Johannine community is with implications that can be drawn from the language of the Gospel. The Fourth Gospel has long been the butt of jokes of Greek scholars because of the "poor" quality of its language. It has been called "primer" Greek, or "schoolhouse" Greek—the sort of language a child might read or even write. Indeed, the simple constructions of most sentences and the limited and repetitive vocabulary make it an ideal choice as a first text for students of Greek to tackle. Alternatively, others have suggested that this is "translation" Greek, reflecting a belated effort to render in Greek a Gospel that was written in another language. They conclude from syntactical structures reminiscent of Semitic languages and from the fact that some Hebrew terms are retained but explained (for example, in 5:2 and 9:7) that the Gospel may have been written—or at least the underlying traditions carried— in Hebrew or Aramaic.

More than translation, however, the language of this Gospel seems to be that of a community in transition, whose current language—in this case, Greek—was not everyone's birth-language. Thus they developed their own unique version of the "new" language that incorporated echoes of the language and culture out of which the elders, at least, had come. The author of this Gospel appears to have been particularly skilled in the use of this blended language that gave voice to the bicultural and perhaps bilingual reality of the community. In short, the language in which the Fourth Gospel was written could be called "immigrant" Greek, not as a pejorative designation, but as one descriptive of the community's liminal place and status.[5]

Such a blend of old and new frequently characterizes the language of communities of people who, after beginning life in one culture and language system, find themselves transplanted into another. They use vocabulary and other aspects of the language of the culture they have joined, but with many grammatical assumptions and language patterns of that from which they have come. The result is that the new language they are beginning to acquire is used without all of the nuances assumed by persons for whom it is their birth language. (For example, this loss of subtle distinctions can be seen in the Fourth Gospel, where the verbs ἀγαπάω and φιλέω are used apparently synonymously.) At the same time the new language may abound with puns or other plays on words that draw on both languages. Contemporary analogies would be the language patterns of many neighborhoods of North American or northern European countries that have become home to persons recently arrived from other regions of the world, where the language, customs, and culture of the home country blend with those of the new country in an amalgam that is neither one nor the other. Subsequent generations usually move toward greater assimilation to the dominant language and culture, until traces of the original disappear or until the new words or expressions find their way into the dominant language. One example of that process in the United States is the "Spanglish" that is spoken by Puerto Ricans living on the U.S. mainland, or by immigrants particularly from Mexico, Central America, or the Spanish-speaking Caribbean. Spanglish is neither bad Spanish nor bad English, but rather a blended language appropriate to the communities who often live (whether by choice or because of racist patterns of housing and employment) in homogeneous communities from which, in most cases, they commute to work in other parts of the city. In the barrios the older immigrants and their U.S.-born children speak a language whose bilingual character heightens people's sense of living in a liminal place between their own homes in Mexico, Puerto Rico, or El Salvador, and their current residence in the United States, and also between their residences and the foreign world that surrounds them.

LOCATION

Where the Johannine community was located is a matter hotly debated among scholars. Geographical details in the Fourth Gospel suggest that this community may have carried a collective memory of pre-70 Palestine, and especially of Jerusalem and Judea, but that this memory can no longer be relied upon to interpret locations of events in the narrative (5:2) or the customs associated with them (9:7).[6] On the other hand, that memory does not appear to be of such long term that such references can be treated casually, or that the emotion associated with them can be dismissed. Along with the precision of such descriptions goes a generally negative attitude toward Jerusalem and persons ideologically identified with its centers of power (in particular the temple) as hostile to Jesus and his followers.[7] Even if that picture goes back to historical memory embedded in the traditions of the community of Jesus' own identification with a Galilean peasant or village community, over against the powerful institutions of the capital city, the fact that it is maintained and even accentuated in the Gospel suggests that such geographical references would still carry meaning for the readers. A number of scholars cite the dualisms that pervade the Gospel to trace the Johannine community's roots to the Qumran community near the Dead Sea. Since, however, Qumran was not the only theological home of dualistic thought, that proposal is hotly debated. Even if some sort of link is granted, the nature of the connection—whether direct participation of early members of John's community at Qumran or second-hand influence through, for example, followers of John the Baptist who joined John's group later—is not clear.[8]

This debate reinforces the observation about the "immigrant language" of the Gospel to suggest a community somewhere in the Jewish Dispersion. The question in 7:35, "Does he intend to go to the Dispersion among the Greeks and teach the Greeks?" is an ironic question on the level of the Gospel community, for that is precisely where the Gospel has moved in the intervening decades.[9] While there are few scholars who locate the community still in Palestine, the others do not agree on where in the Diaspora it may have been situated. A city with a Jewish population is most likely, given the apparent location of a synagogue there. Having said that, however, raises more questions than it answers. The existence of at least one synagogue says nothing about the size of the Jewish community, nor of its theological orientation among the diversity that still existed in the late first century. That diversity would have been enhanced in the Diaspora as Judaism—like the various forms of nascent Christianity—blended with various expressions and values of the surrounding culture. Ephesus is the city that receives the strongest support among scholars as the home of the Fourth Gospel, though most recognize that earlier generations of the community would have made other stops, picking up influences from various Christian and Jewish groups all along the way.[10]

Alexandria is also sometimes mentioned as a possible place of origin. Arguing in its favor is the early appearance there of a papyrus copy of the Fourth Gospel (P[52], dating from 135 C.E.),[11] the presence of not only a Jewish community, but also a highly dualistic Jewish theology in the writings of Philo, and the prominence there of wisdom language and Wisdom traditions.[12] In addition, the distance of Alexandria from other Christian centers in Asia Minor fits with the distinctive voice of this Gospel that reflects neither the pastoral concerns of the post-Pauline letters of the same time period (in particular, issues of church order, ethical conformity, or an emerging theological orthodoxy), nor literary dependence on the Synoptic Gospels. Although, in the final analysis, one's conclusion about the geographic location of this community has no great effect on one's interpretation of the Gospel, arguments in favor of Alexandria seem to me the most persuasive.

SOCIAL COMPOSITION

Ethnicity

The ethnic composition of the Johannine community is suggested by a number of clues in the narrative. A combination of interpretations of Jesus by appeal to Hebrew Scriptures (though with less frequent actual quotation than in the Synoptic Gospels[13]), the evident importance to John's community of participation in the synagogue, the ambiguity about the meaning of οἱ Ἰουδαῖοι against whom such hostility is expressed, and the generally Semitic character of the Greek in which the Gospel was written points to a core of the community being ethnically and religiously Jewish Christians[14]—although, as the discussion below makes clear, discerning what that general label might mean is itself a problem. The narrative prominence of the disciples of John the Baptist as the first disciples who come to Jesus may also suggest the continuing prominence of that strand of Jewish reformers in John's community.

The story of the Samaritan woman, which ends with the report that many Samaritans had come to recognize Jesus as "truly the Savior of the world" (4:39–42), provides another narrative clue to the ethnic composition of the Johannine community. Exactly what role, if any, Samaritans may have played is less clear, for they are not mentioned again in the Gospel as being among Jesus' followers. The prominence of this narrative as the first story of the spread of the message about Jesus by one who herself had come to follow him does highlight Samaritans in a positive way. In addition, in 8:48 Jesus is attacked by his opponents (οἱ Ἰουδαῖοι) as a Samaritan and as having a demon. The reply, "I do not have a demon," leaves the charge of being a Samaritan unanswered. While that does not mean that Jesus was accepting that identity (and indeed, in 4:9 the Samaritan woman herself calls him a Ἰουδαῖος), it does imply that the label does not carry the stigma that it did among many Jews. Brown concludes from the evidence in the text that the addition of Samaritans (among other groups) to the original followers of Jesus who became the Johannine community might be responsible for beginning the expansion of Johannine christological categories beyond those drawn from the Hebrew Scriptures and found in the call story of 1:35–51.[15]

The reference in 12:20–26 to the inclusion of some "Greeks" among Jesus' followers in a process parallel to the call of the first disciples (1:35–51) suggests the presence of another group in the Johannine community. Despite the suggestions of some scholars that this might be the author's way of referring to the presence in the Johannine community of Hellenized Diaspora Jews, the most likely reference is to Gentiles whose specific origin is undetermined.[16] A striking factor is that there is no hint that the Johannine community experienced any of the tension around circumcision or food laws that seems to have marked the coexistence of Jews and Gentiles in other Christian communities, such as the Pauline churches. Rather than indicating the absence of Gentiles, that silence most likely indicates either a later period when such questions of practice had been resolved and doctrinal issues were paramount, or else a Jewish community not characterized by meticulous attention to such laws. Common sense indicates that there would have been contact with Gentiles in any Jewish community in a Diaspora city, or even in Palestine under Roman rule, so to imagine the presence of non-Jews in the Johannine community is not difficult. On the other hand, it is impossible to identify evidence in this Gospel of direct influence of the Hellenistic world not filtered first through Judaism,[17] and (unlike other Christian communities of the first century) there is no evidence discernible in the text itself that the Johannine community undertook a deliberate mission to Gentiles.[18] Obviously such a mission occurred with the use of this Gospel. It was likely abetted in a negative way by the apparently anti-Jewish language of the Gospel, and in a positive way by the author's use of theological and christological categories that communicated Jesus' importance even to people who were not formed by the traditions of the Hebrew Scriptures.

While we cannot know for certain that the Johannine community included Samaritans and Gentiles, their explicit incorporation among Jesus' followers in the Gospel's narrative suggests that these groups were important either to the memory or to the present composition of that community. An additional support for this suggestion about the multiethnic composition of the community can be seen in the explanations provided for the meaning and observance of the various festivals that mark the narrative time of the first half of the Gospel. The festivals are thus "baptized" into the Christian story by their connection to events in Jesus' life—a move that would have been important to those in the community who knew and observed those festivals as part of their pre-Christian religious life. At the same time, those who had not been accustomed to observing these festivals would be introduced to their importance and prepared for the ongoing role of their replacement forms in the life of the Johannine community.[19]

Gender

Nothing in the Gospel provides explicit information about women's roles and place in the Johannine community. Women do, however, figure prominently in the Gospel narrative. That literary evidence about attitudes toward women is ambiguous. The number of women characters is rather small, but they play key roles in the unfolding drama. The request of the (unnamed) mother of Jesus prompts the first of the "signs" (2:11–12) and moves Jesus toward the ultimate σημεῖον of the cross on which he will be "lifted up" (3:13–15). The Samaritan woman in John 4 is the first person actually described as carrying the message about Jesus to her community. She does so on the heels of a multilayered theological discussion about appropriate worship, Jewish and Samaritan understandings of purity laws, and the role of Jacob as ancestor. Mary and Martha are involved in Jesus' raising of their brother, the episode that triggers the final burst of hostility against Jesus. Martha voices the model confession of Jesus as the Christ (11:27) that the Synoptics attribute to Peter. Her confession, like the coming to faith of the Samaritan woman, comes on the heels of a theological discussion, this time about resurrection. Her sister Martha's confession is expressed in action, as she models the foot washing (12:1–8) that Jesus subsequently identifies as the appropriate action of the disciples toward one another (13:12–17). A group of women is listed as witnesses to Jesus' death (19:25). Mary Magdalene is identified as the first to see the risen Christ (20:11–18), and she carries the message of Jesus' resurrection to the other disciples.[20] While the prominence of these roles cannot be denied, it must be recognized that none of these women appears in more than two episodes of the Gospel. In contrast, various male characters do have recurring roles (Peter, Andrew, Thomas, Philip, and Nicodemus, for example).[21] To conclude on this evidence that the narrative itself points to egalitarian patterns of leadership in the community[22] might be stretching the data, but there is other evidence to consider that might lend support to such a conclusion.

Clearly the most prominent character in the Gospel other than Jesus is the unnamed "disciple whom Jesus loved." The anonymity of that key character on whose testimony the whole Gospel is said to depend (21:24) has made the identity of that figure a topic of debate. Some scholars have resolved the issue by concluding that this is really a composite or model disciple and not a specific character in the Gospel. The active role of this character who appears throughout the last half of the Gospel (13:23; 19:26; 20:2; 21:7, 20) suggests that one ought at least to explore whether a specific person can be identified.[23] Ecclesiastical tradition has identified that disciple with John of Zebedee, who does not appear as a character in this Gospel. The argument goes that the Synoptic Gospels make his presence among Jesus' followers obvious, and the fact that the beloved disciple is unnamed reflects John's role here not as actor, but as witness. Many members of Jesus' community of followers remain unnamed, however, and such an argument from silence lacks persuasiveness.

Another route is to ask whether any of the characters who are identified as part of the narrative would fit the description "the disciple whom Jesus loved." In fact, the three characters said explicitly to be loved by Jesus are the family from Bethany (11:5). The evident intimacy between that family and Jesus makes them good candidates. Lazarus has indeed been suggested, under the assumption—based both on patriarchal tradition and on the reference to this person as "son" in 19:26—that this disciple is a male.

Two of the three members of the "beloved" family, however, are women—Mary and Martha—who have central roles in the identification of Jesus and his significance for the believers. The question thus must be raised whether this one whose testimony is the foundation of the Gospel and of this community could be a woman. Since the word for disciple (μαθητής) is grammatically masculine without a (known) feminine parallel, that word itself does not indicate the gender of the person to whom it refers. More problematic is 19:26, where the dying Jesus is said to call this disciple his mother's "son" (υἱός). The previous verse lists Jesus' mother among a number of other women standing near the cross. Without mentioning the arrival of any other person, the narrator continues with a reference to "his mother and the disciple whom he loved standing beside her." While the gender of the word υἱός is unambiguous in its reference to a "son" and not a "daughter" (θυγάτηρ), two factors mitigate its force as proof that this disciple must be seen as a male. The first is the responsibility assigned to this person: care of the mother of a friend who is dying. According to a number of popular Hellenistic philosophers whose discussions might well have been part of the cultural context of John's community, one of the principal duties of a friend was to take on the filial and other familial responsibilities of a friend who was dying or at risk of death (see the discussion in chapter 5, below). In other words, the friend becomes a substitute "son" of the family. That is what happens here. Additionally, using a masculine noun, even if the "real" referent was a woman, would have enhanced the credibility of the community's unique witness to Jesus in a church increasingly marked by the patriarchalism and hierarchalism of the surrounding Roman society (as the pastoral epistles make perfectly clear).

In the final analysis, the "disciple whom Jesus loved" is still anonymous, but at least the possibility exists that this disciple might have been a woman. Add that possibility to the accounts of specific women who play key roles in the Gospel's narrative, and a picture emerges of a community that—like a number of the synagogues of this period[24]—may have centered around a woman's leadership and grounded its theology on the testimony of her powerful sisters. Unfortunately, whether such leadership would have persisted as late as the end of the first century when the Gospel was written is unknown. Like the question of community leadership, the question of authorship also remains unresolved. Even if the witness whose testimony provided the traditions about Jesus was a woman, there is nothing in the final form of the Gospel to suggest the gender of the author who gave those traditions (and the community's subsequent reflection on them) their final shape.

Economic Status

The Gospel itself provides few clues to the social or economic status of the hearers. Absent is the overt proclamation of good news to the poor that characterizes the preaching of Jesus according to the Synoptic tradition, and missing too are the stock characters of social criticism that one encounters in the Synoptic parables. Wes Howard-Brook concludes from that silence that the Johannine community "was probably a relatively prosperous group."[25] He notes, however, that the narrative clue that "the poor" are present within the community as well (12:8; cf. 9:40; 18:5, 18) suggests that a mix of economic classes comprise the community.

One can, however, reconstruct a bias of this Gospel in favor of those who would have been the marginalized people — "the poor" — of their society that is parallel to the better known bias of the Synoptic Gospels. That bias can be seen in healing stories, which bring into focus the circumstances of persons marginalized from daily life by their illness (4:46–54), blindness (9:1–41), or paralysis (5:1–18). Even Nicodemus, who with Joseph of Arimathea represent the economic and religious elite of their society, moves toward participation in the Johannine community in a way that relinquishes the privilege and protection his position afforded.[26]

Jesus is thus portrayed as the one who mediates healing to people on the margins of society, restoring them to active involvement where before they have been passive observers. Furthermore, for those whose marginalization is a consequence of their discipleship, becoming Jesus' disciples is itself sufficient motive and support. The healing stories in John 5 and 9 have the ambiguous effect of exposing the healed persons to the need as well as the possibility of obeying laws affecting principally able-bodied people, and when they failed, exposing them to the criticisms of religious authorities. Even through such stories with their social referents, however, the healing message of the gospel for this community seems to be directed to the pain of religious marginalization in particular, as the community proclaimed the redemptive presence that was strong enough even to overcome their experience or fear of exclusion from the synagogue.

THE JOHANNINE COMMUNITY
AND οἱ Ἰουδαῖοι

The strength of the positive references to Jewish traditions and symbols and the vitriolic attack against οἱ Ἰουδαῖοι in the Fourth Gospel suggest that an examination of that term, and of the relationship of the Johannine community to those to whom that term refers, provides additional clues to the reconstruction of the implied audience of that Gospel.

The Jesus proclaimed by the Fourth Gospel is the man from Nazareth (1:45–46), a regular traveler on the roads linking Galilee and Jerusalem, participant in various Jewish festivals, addressed as "rabbi," and interpreted in categories drawn from the

Hebrew Scriptures.[27] Like divine Wisdom who seeks those who will follow wisdom's path (Prov. 8:2–3), Jesus encounters many of those who come to believe in him on the street corners and byways of that same world of Roman-occupied Palestine. He and they make frequent visits to Jerusalem and find their religious center in the temple and its surrounding culture. In the most elaborately described encounter between Jesus and someone who is not Jewish, the woman from Samaria repeatedly identifies Jesus as a Jew (4:7–25), and no reader would question the accuracy of her judgment.

The narrator, however, clearly distinguishes Jesus from οἱ Ἰουδαῖοι—a term most English translations render as "the Jews" (see, for example, 5:16, 18; 6:41; 7:1; 10:31; 11:8, 54). Although the hostility implied, or even overtly expressed, by this group toward Jesus is a striking aspect of the Fourth Gospel, the term can be used without hostile connotations as well. (A festival can be identified as τῶν Ἰουδαίων, for example.)[28] It is thus evident that in the Fourth Gospel that term does not reliably refer to the religio-ethnic community usually understood from its English equivalent.[29] An argument could be made that in this Gospel the term should be translated as "the Judeans"—people from the area around Jerusalem connected in a variety of ways to the political, economic, and religious hegemony of the temple that Jesus opposed (2:13–22).[30] That opposition could well be understood as an economic and social struggle internal to the Jewish population of Palestine. Jesus took a stand against an exploitative economic system that harmed both poor urban dwellers and the residents of rural Galilee—groups whom the Johannine and Synoptic traditions alike say that Jesus defended. The "area" of οἱ Ἰουδαῖοι thus indicates a social and ideological location, as well as the geographical places—Jerusalem and its environs—where Jesus encounters hostility. This area is in stark contrast to hospitable Galilee, where the bread of life can be shared in safety (6:1–14).[31]

More than a historical reference to Jesus' life and to literal Galilee and Judea seems to be at stake, given the striking repetition of the term οἱ Ἰουδαῖοι throughout the Gospel (even where it seems almost gratuitous to the narrative being developed) and the narrative energy expended to emphasize the hostility of that group to Jesus and his followers. The term apparently also had symbolic meaning and perhaps a contemporary referent for the Johannine community. The power of this term for that community is suggested by bringing together two clues provided by the author. First, "separation from the synagogue" is presented as a threat to the followers of Jesus (9:22; 12:42; 16:2). Second, οἱ Ἰουδαῖοι are portrayed as those who might enforce this threat against members of John's community, just as they also represent the principal source of hostility to Jesus. Thus, on one level, the term "the religious authorities" might seem to be an appropriate way to render the term. On the other hand, sometimes οἱ Ἰουδαῖοι does not refer to the leaders but makes general reference to the Jewish people as a whole. Consequently, that term solves neither the problem of translation nor that of interpretation.[32] Perhaps, though, the confusion surrounding the translation of the term is itself a helpful aspect of Johannine interpretation, because it underlines the fact that "the Jews," like other ethnic groups, were not monolithic in their response to Jesus or, in fact, in other aspects of their life and identity. Some Jews believed in Jesus and became followers of his way; others who experienced him and his way as a threat to their life and their religion were hostile to him and to all connected with him; probably the largest majority took no stand for or against him or the movement—later the church—that took shape because of him.[33]

In a landmark study that has, with some variations, come to represent a near consensus among Johannine scholars, J. Louis Martyn[34] connected the texts referring to that threat with actions attributed to a gathering at Jamnia in which leaders of the Jewish community proposed a variety of means to interpret the recent sacking of Jerusalem and of the temple by the Romans, and to establish guidelines for Jewish life in the new period inaugurated by that tragic event. Among those actions, according to Martyn, were liturgical revisions that included changes in the *Birkath haMinim,* or Benediction against the Heretics. In its new form, so the argument goes, the Benedictions could be used both to identify and subsequently to expel from the synagogue any Jews who were believers in "the Nazarene." Such action would have been part of the process of clarification of criteria for Jewish identity and practice suitable to the new context when the focal point of the temple was gone and when the many expressions of Jewish religion that flourished in the earlier period in Palestine and the Diaspora alike could no longer be as easily tolerated. According to Martyn's argument, this action was both a consequence of and a crucial step toward the establishment of the rabbis of Jamnia as the principal spokespersons for Judaism, and in setting the course toward the ultimate recognition of "rabbinic Judaism" as normative.

While it is generally agreed that some sort of expulsion from the synagogue marked the experience of the Johannine community, specific details of Martyn's hypothesis have been challenged. For example, some scholars have questioned whether the Benediction against the Heretics was the specific device for invoking the ban. A number question whether that prayer had been revised to target specifically Christians (and not all manner of heterodox or, better put, heteropraxis Jews) by the last decades of the first century. Others question the enforceability of the Benedictions as part of a policy applicable in all synagogues. Perhaps, some suggest, Johannine Christians just happened to be the targets in their community of a more general effort to limit diversity in post-70 Judaism. Or perhaps a device like the Benediction happened to be used in that locale against these Christians, but there was not a system-wide opposition between Judaism and Christianity, or, more specifically, between church and synagogue. Whatever the variations, the near consensus continues to posit some sort of historical event in which Johannine Christians were forcibly separated from the synagogue or synagogues in which they wanted to continue to be involved. According to this reconstruction, the hostility to "the Jews" expressed in the narrative of the Gospel reflects that experience of opposition, and the Gospel itself is designed in part to assuage the pain of that separation.

Several problems surround this set of reconstructions, accounting for some of their variety and finally calling into question the underlying thesis. First, the date when the *Birkath haMinim* was revised to target especially Christians is unclear, and may well have been much later than the time of composition of the Gospel. Second, whether that liturgical expression actually carried with it a formal institutional or community ban is also a matter of debate, since the key word underlying the hypothesis, ἀποσυνάγωγος, may convey a static condition indicating that one is separate from the synagogue, or it may have an active sense that indicates removal or motion away from the synagogue. Third, whether in the last quarter of the first century any central group within Judaism would have been viewed as having enough authority to effect such an act and to impose it upon Jews elsewhere is doubtful. A fourth problem is the set of unknowns surrounding the reference to the synagogue. What participation in the synagogue entailed for the community from which the Johannine Christians emerged is totally unknown, whether in terms of practices or activities or in terms of the theological orientation of Judaism that predominated. It is usually assumed that if the threat of separation from the synagogue was seen negatively by John's community, the synagogue must have been important to everyone in the Jewish community of that city from which the Johannine community came; but that is not necessarily the case. Even less reliable is the assumption that, after the fall of the temple at Jerusalem, participation in a synagogue was foundational to the life of all Jews. What people did in the synagogue and how synagogue activities shaped the community's life in homes, in the market, in places of business, or in their relationship to the surrounding society are all unknown factors. The assumption apparently underlying most scholarly reconstructions is that the synagogue was a community nearly identical to modern synagogues—a house of study, prayer, and related community life. That description does not necessarily hold true, however, for all or even any synagogues of John's context.

A related question is what criteria separated the Johannine Christians from the synagogue community. Of the issues stated or implied in Paul's letters and in the Synoptic Gospels to stand as the principal points of difference between followers of Jesus and other Jews (circumcision, food laws, and sabbath observance), the only one mentioned in the Fourth Gospel is sabbath observance (chapter 5). In none of the other extant Christian texts of the first century is sabbath observance identified as a distinguishing factor by which people were weeded out of the synagogue. The reason for expulsion given in the Gospel—belief in Jesus as healer or even as messiah—by itself is nowhere else cited as a major problem for non-believing Jews.[35] Perhaps the particular Christology of this community opened them to charges of ditheism, or at least of considering Jesus to be equal to God (5:18). Perhaps the problem lay in the related issue of the authority of Jesus and his followers to discern the will of God (5:19–30). It is possible that some such affirmation made the community's belief itself, and not the usual criteria of practice, determinative for the relationship of Johannine Christians to the synagogue in this case.[36] At the very least, the Jewish affirmation of a religion centered on God mediated by Torah, land, and people has been replaced in this Gospel by the Christian confession of Christ as the place—in fact, the only place—where God can be encountered and known.[37]

A final uncertainty in Martyn's reconstruction is the assumption that the fall of Jerusalem and the destruction of the temple would have traumatized the Jewish community of which the Johannine community had been a part. If, as seems apparent, they were already a community in a city of the Diaspora, their practice of their religion would already have evolved in a way that was not tied to the temple liturgy. Despite the symbolic importance of Jerusalem in the Hebrew Scriptures and despite the emotional attachment to the city for a community composed principally of people only a generation or two removed from Palestine, it does not necessarily follow that the loss of the temple would have evoked dramatic actions to purify and redefine the Jewish community of the Diaspora city where John's community was located.

In addition to such problems in the historical reconstruction undergirding the Martyn hypothesis, it is important to note that expulsion by the leaders of the synagogue is not the only explanation that would account for the posture of the Fourth Gospel against οἱ Ἰουδαῖοι or the language of opposition found in the narrative.[38] Despite references to believers in Jesus being "put out of the synagogue" (9:22; 12:42; 16:2), that language comes from the Johannine community. It names their experience of exclusion, but not necessarily in the terms the parent community would have used to describe the same circumstances. For instance, what occurred may be analogous to what happens in modern churches and synagogues when a group in the congregation—perhaps beginning at a retreat or conference and sustained in continued meetings afterward—experiences a style of worship, theology, spirituality, or other practice different from that of their home community. At some point they try to convince others in the congregation to join them in their new way. A few do, but the majority judges the new way not to be consistent with the congregation's traditions of belief or practice. The congregation and its leaders may well urge the group to continue their exploration and to meet together to support and encourage one another, but remain firm in their decision not to make the new way the governing mode of the congregation. The group championing their new ways, however, often interprets such a decision as rejection and exclusion. As the story of the surrounding events is told and retold, the leaders of the parent congregation are portrayed as the enemy. The group's experience is of expulsion, rejection, even persecution. Were the parent community to tell the story, however, they would utterly deny having taken any such punitive action and would affirm that they definitely still consider the dissidents as a part of the community.[39]

When a group feels rejected by the larger congregation in which it originated, that group often reinterprets the history it shares with the parent community as well. That reinterpretation of the tradition of the congregation aims to prove that the members of the dissident group are indeed the true representatives of their religion.[40] The rupture in the immediate relationship in no way entails the rejection of the common history. On the contrary, the group that has separated itself builds a significant support for its new identity on a sort of narrative supercessionism, in which their version of that history places them at the center and the position of the parent congregation is seen as divergent.

In addition to these modern analogies, a significant detail within the Gospel narrative itself suggests caution in characterizing both the nature of the relationship between the Johannine community and the parent synagogue and the cause of the apparent tension. That detail is the presence of οἱ Ἰουδαῖοι paying what amounts to a pastoral call on the grieving sisters from Bethany (11:31).[41] If there were an expulsion directed against those who believe in Jesus, certainly these close friends would have felt its sting. Given Martha's confession of Jesus as "the Messiah, the Son of God, the one coming into the world" (11:27), which directly parallels the "great Confession" of Peter in the Synoptics (Matt. 16:16//Mark 8:29//Luke 9:20), the sisters' inclusion among the followers of Jesus is not coincidental. In fact, they serve as paradigmatic representatives of the Johannine community. The Gospel narrative, however, portrays them as very much within the purview of the synagogue leaders (at least from the perspective of those leaders), whatever the Johannine community's experience of that relationship may have been. One question that must be raised to this reading of John 11, however, is whether the sisters' new status as a household of women following Lazarus's death affected the way they would have been viewed by the leaders of the synagogue. Perhaps in their new status, they were not worth the trouble of exclusion and no longer to be taken seriously. Despite the persistence of such manifestations of patriarchy, however, its history through the centuries of the Christian church suggests that, while women were often not taken seriously, when they espoused divergent religious beliefs and practices, instead of being treated more charitably than men, they often were (and still are) punished even more severely.

JOHN AND THE SYNOPTIC GOSPELS

A final dimension of the identity of this community that must be considered is its relationship to other Christian groups of its day. In the middle decades of the twentieth century, the focal issue in Johannine scholarship was the "Gnostic" voice of the Gospel. Subsequent study has made it clear that the question contained an anachronism, in that Christian Gnosticism appeared later. The Fourth Gospel thus could have been neither espousing nor combatting Gnostics. In fact, the language of that Gospel provided a rich resource in the subsequent evolution of the various forms of Gnostic thought.[42]

Discerning the relationship between the Johannine community and other New Testament churches of the late first century is more complex, in part because of the diversity represented in what was once identified as the emerging "catholic" church. The voices of the pastoral epistles, with their concerns for church order, doctrine, discipline, and qualifications for office speak a language foreign to this Gospel, which uses only "disciple" and eventually "friend" to designate Jesus' followers as an undifferentiated group. The Gospel's doctrinal claims rely on the authority of its own source, "the disciple whom Jesus loved," rather than on an ecclesiastical endorsement. Questions of internal discipline revolve around the need for solidarity in the face of hostility from outside, rather than on a need to limit divergence from a norm. One can detect in the Fourth Gospel neither opposition to the voices of the pastorals nor support for them, but rather those two branches of the Christian movement appear not to intersect at all.

The issue is different relative to the churches from which the Synoptic Gospels emerged. While it is impossible to argue for specific occasions of interaction between those churches and the Johannine community, their common project of Gospel writing and the patterns of similarity in the overall design and in the details of the Gospels provide at least the basis for a discussion. Taken together, these clues further establish the identity of the Johannine community among the variety of early Christian groups and narrow the focus on its time and place of origin.

The fact that the Fourth Gospel is centered on the person of Jesus and his christological significance establishes this as a Christian document. While that might seem self-evident to modern readers, apparently John felt constrained to establish that point, particularly relative to John the Baptist. The early introduction of John (1:6) echoes the Synoptics in linking John to the beginning of Jesus' ministry (Matt. 3:1–17//Mark 1:2–11//Luke 3:1–22//John 1:19–34). The author of the Fourth Gospel, however, takes care to establish John not primarily as forerunner and preparer of the way of "the Lord." Rather, in this Gospel John is first of all a "witness" (1:7), whose job is to testify to Jesus and to lead others to him (1:35). An important clue to the context of the Johannine community, then, is that it is focused on Jesus and not John, and that—perhaps even more than in the communities to which the Synoptic Gospels were addressed—that point cannot be taken for granted, but must be established by clear narrative argument.

The rhythm of similarities and differences marks any discussion of the relationship between the Fourth Gospel and the Synoptics. On the one hand, this book looks like a Gospel (even though neither the noun εὐαγγέλιον nor the verb εὐαγγελίζομαι is found in it) in that, like the Synoptic Gospels, it presents the life and teachings of Jesus in an apparent biographical form.[43] It includes accounts of healings and other wondrous deeds, as well as teachings attributed to him, and it zooms to a close focus on events of the final days of Jesus' life, on his death, and on reports of his resurrection. On the other hand, within that overall similarity the Fourth Gospel differs from the Synoptics on a number of points. For example, this Gospel does not contain accounts of Jesus as an exorcist who demonstrates authority over "demons" and other "powers" of the liminal world between the human and the divine. His teachings take the form of long addresses instead of the sort of brief sayings and parables that mark the Synoptic traditions. Except for the similes of the vine (John 15) and the shepherd (John 10), Jesus' teachings lack the specific references to pastoral scenes and rural life so common in the Synoptic parables (for example, sowing and harvesting, and problems related to absentee landlords). The Fourth Gospel differs also in the chronology and sequence in which events of the story are presented. Thus, Jesus' action against the commercial center surrounding the Jerusalem temple is narrated early in the story (John 2), instead of as a part of the events of Jesus' final week. Jesus and his followers are said to make several trips to Jerusalem in the course of his public ministry, instead of the single pilgrimage to the place and events of his death as the Synoptics tell the story. The death itself is said by John to have occurred on the eve of the Passover instead of during the festival as the Synoptics suggest. By means of that difference in chronological detail, the death of the one called "lamb of God" (1:29, 36) is set at the same hour when the Passover lambs would have been slaughtered. At the same time, with that shift in chronology the account of the final evening of Jesus with the disciples is taken up not with the meal that provides the foundation for the Christian sacrament of the Lord's Supper, but rather with the dramatic example of Jesus' washing of the disciples' feet. The interpretation of the broken bread is linked in this Gospel to the account of Jesus' feeding of the crowds in Galilee in John 6. The group of "the Twelve" receive little mention in John as leaders among the disciples[44]—a role that is prominent in the Synoptics. Mention of an inner circle of disciples (Peter, James, and John) and the title ἀπόστολος are both missing, in contrast to their prominence in the Synoptics—all this, despite the prominence in the Fourth Gospel of the designation of the "sent one" to refer to Jesus (for which forms of the verbs ἀποστέλλω and πέμπω are used interchangeably) and to the disciples as well (17:18; 20:21).

Such similarities and differences imply either a community whose history since the time of Jesus has been independent of the communities addressed in the Synoptic Gospels, or at the very least a community that did not feel bound to conform its proclamation of Jesus to that found in the other Gospels.[45] Nothing in the language of the text itself suggests that the author of the Fourth Gospel used the other Gospels or even shared sources in common with them. For example, while all four Gospels attribute healings to Jesus, the healing stories in John do not echo any of those found in the Synoptics. Even the passion narrative, where the parallels between the Fourth Gospel and the other Gospels are closest, exhibits significant differences in emphasis and lacks the sort of verbal similarity that leads to the conclusion that the authors shared common written or even well-developed oral sources.

Among the teachings attributed to Jesus, only two sayings found in John echo ones found in the Synoptics with sufficient precision to raise the question of dependency (compare, for example, John 4:44 with Matt. 13:57//Mark 6:4//Luke 4:24; and John 12:25 with Matt. 16:25; 10:39//Mark 8:35//Luke 9:24; 17:33). The first of these is the sort of proverbial expression that it could well have been simply a cultural artifact common to the Gospel traditions. The second, which is attested in both Mark and the additional source shared by Matthew and Luke as well as in John, is so striking in its contradiction of common sense and popular wisdom that it may well represent a remembered saying of Jesus preserved in the traditions reported by John's source as well as in the oral traditions underlying the Synoptic sources.

The Fourth Gospel itself claims to trace its account of Jesus to "the disciple whom Jesus loved" (21:20–25) and acknowledges that, while the account is true, it is not the whole truth (in the sense of all that might be said) about Jesus (20:30–31; 21:25). By that closing comment, the author both makes room for the legitimate existence of different Gospels and lodges the claim to this as an authoritative account on the firm ground of the relationship between Jesus and "the disciple who is testifying to these things." Whether it is possible to identify this source with a specific person, or whether the rather elliptical designation as "the one whom Jesus loved" is intended to refer to an ideal or symbolic figure, is unclear. If indeed the beloved one refers to a follower of Jesus, as I noted earlier, the three named followers who are specifically said to be loved by Jesus are the family from Bethany—Mary, Martha, and Lazarus (11:5).

One scenario, then, for identifying the Johannine community is to understand it as tracing its connection to Jesus to an early community gathered around one or more members of this family. That community's history may at times have intertwined with the life of other Christian communities whose links to Jesus were through the sources gathered in the Synoptic traditions; but, basically, it followed a distinct but not separate course.[46] The ambivalence of that distinction-without-separation is especially clear in the diminished role of Peter prior to the passion narrative, in comparison to his role in the Synoptic Gospels. Where he does appear—in the sequence of call stories (1:42), at the interpretation of the bread of life (6:68), and at the foot washing just before Jesus' arrest (13:6–10)—the narrative moments undergird concerns of the church's leadership or its worship, which were connected to Peter in the Synoptic traditions, and presumably in the churches from which they came. Similarly, Peter's appearances with the "disciple whom Jesus loved" as a witness to the empty tomb and as one charged by the risen Christ to become a "good shepherd" to the sheep (21:15–19) stand as ecumenical overtures to the church that acclaimed Peter as the principal pastoral authority.

Just as the communities shaped by the foundational Gospel of Mark and by the various collections of sayings and other materials of the Synoptic traditions continued to reshape and adapt their materials to keep the Gospel relevant to their changing communities, so also the Johannine community likely kept the treasured memories from the one whom Jesus loved and refocused those traditions through years of changing circumstances and needs. In other words, the Johannine community appears to have replicated much of the process of development of its Gospel that attended the development of the Synoptic Gospels. The motivation to move from remembered traditions about Jesus into a written Gospel appears to have come in all the communities as a consequence of the passage of time, the need to preserve the memories before they could be lost, and the need to establish limits to the process of interpretation and adaptation of the traditions in order to provide norms for the communities' life in the wake of a variety of changes such as the incorporation of new converts and migration into and throughout the Diaspora, and in response to the pressure of events and groups outside the community. These factors suggest a date in the last quarter of the first century—a suggestion consistent with manuscript evidence.[47]

To speak, then, of "the disciple whom Jesus loved" as the source of the Fourth Gospel's traditions about Jesus does not identify that person with the anonymous author of the Fourth Gospel. The author appears to have been a leader and spokesperson to and for the community in the final decades of the first century who drew on the traditions about Jesus (which may well have come from "the disciple whom Jesus loved") and the community's history of remembering and interpreting those traditions, in order to read them all again in the community's new context.[48] The author thus gives voice to the history of the community's reflection on the memories of Jesus that founded it, and to their retelling of that story that shaped the intervening history of the community from which this Gospel came and to which it was directed.[49]

CONCLUSION

To weave together the threads of these disjointed clues into the fabric of the Johannine community requires the supplying of some—though I hope minimal—

connective strands. The resulting picture suggests a small community living probably in the Jewish sector of a Diaspora city in the final quarter of the first century.
Consistent with such a location, the community appears to have included a core of
Jewish members, but also Samaritans and Gentiles who needed to be brought on
board through the explanation of various Jewish practices (notably, the observance
of the various festivals). The synagogue appears to have been at the heart of the
religious life of the community from which the core of the Johannine community
came, given the fact that being "removed" from the synagogue—whatever that actually meant to those who continued in the synagogue—expresses the community's perception of a threat to which it would be subject because of its faith in
Jesus. The core of the community may be descendants of an immigrant community with strong ties to and lively memories of Palestine in general, and of Jerusalem in particular. But at least some of the current members required the
explanation of Hebrew terms and of place names. That would suggest that they
were not unlike second generations of immigrants in all ages who live on a linguistic and cultural bridge between their community of origin and the culture of
their present place of residence. The community appears to have been made up
largely of people who were not a part of the leadership group of their community
of origin, though apparently at least some of the leaders (reflected narratively in
such characters as Nicodemus and Joseph of Arimathea) also were believers. The
community clearly was experiencing a tension that related to some sort of split between the Johannine community and the parent synagogue, but what caused that
split, or who initiated it, is not clear. Nevertheless, that event appears to be the principal lens through which the story of Jesus is refracted, leading to its focus on the
internal life of the community and on Jesus' role in providing comfort, healing,
and support as the specific definition of the more abstract term "salvation." As a
consequence, the community does not exhibit much interest in such churchly concerns as mission and evangelism.[50] It is focused on itself and questions of its survival.

The picture we get is of a community fighting for its own integrity by setting itself over against—and yet still connected to—other Christians (such as the
churches of the Synoptic tradition), and also over against such outsiders as the followers of John the Baptist and the community's principal antagonists, "the Jews."
In addition to such external boundary questions, the community appears to have
worked on internal issues of identity by clarifying its beliefs and founding stories
about Jesus.[51] Few clues are given about the internal life or organization of this
community. The long discourse on the bread of life in John 6 suggests that a shared
meal was part of the life of this community, as it was of the life of other early Christian communities. Perhaps the example of servanthood in the foot washing by Jesus
(13:1–12) also found its way into the symbol system as well as the liturgical life of
the community. The attention paid to Jewish festivals would suggest that the community observed a Christianized version of these festivals. The absence of such formal titles as "apostle" or of the centrality of any single group of Jesus' followers
suggests a more charismatic than institutionalized leadership pattern. Instead of
such titles, the presence of the Holy Spirit as the παράκλητος is the key to the con-

tinuation of Jesus' ministry according to the Fourth Gospel. What the long-term effect of such a view of the basis of leadership might have had on the structure and life of the community is unclear.

At the time when the Gospel was written, there is no evidence of division or unrest within the community. The love commandment (15:12–17), and not formal offices or orders, was to be the key to their survival and faithfulness alike in the face of the external threats it experienced. In the Johannine letters, however, it is clear that internal debates and divisions began to be revealed concerning beliefs as well as practice. The grand dream of the community organized around love simply did not survive in the waking hours of community life.

Chapter 3

The Roots of Wisdom

The word "wisdom" is mentioned nowhere in the Fourth Gospel (or the Johannine letters, for that matter). Establishing the centrality of this motif, then, requires that we begin by identifying the theological dimensions of wisdom found among the traditions available to members of this community to express their confession of Jesus as the Christ. The literature and world view of Hellenistic Judaism form the matrix from which wisdom emerged as a central theological motif in the Fourth Gospel.

At its most basic level, in the theocentric world view of the Hebrew Bible and the religions that depended on it, wisdom is connected to the divine logic undergirding the creation—God's will or plan for the created order and for the deep structures and relationships that give the world meaning, shape, and coherence. That evidence of wisdom in the creation itself, in turn, reflects God's own nature. Wisdom thus names a bridge between Creator and creation. The divine nature traverses that bridge into the world of nature and into the human social and ethical orders alike, and wisdom names both the end and the means of humankind's relationship to God.

In the literature of Judaism that antedates the Gospel of John, wisdom is encountered in the section of the Hebrew Bible called the "Writings" or *Kethuvim* (in Job, Psalms, and especially in Proverbs); in Sirach, Baruch, and the Wisdom of Solomon, which are included among the deuterocanonical books of the Christian canon; in the apocalyptic books of *1 Enoch* and *2 Esdras;* and in the writings of Philo. Together these writings constitute a theological complex connected to the rest of the Hebrew Bible in its theocentric nature, but focused through the lenses of creation and society. Wisdom literature seeks to discern and describe the order inherent in the structures of society that give shape to human life: God's ways are known in the order of the world itself. The very premise of wisdom literature lies in the centrality of language to cultural traditions and even to human existence. It draws both on folk traditions indigenous to a variety of cultures (on proverbs, folktales, and legends) and on the cosmopolitan concerns and media of royal courts.[1]

Wisdom literature acquires its particular focus due to the stresses of life in various moments of the postexilic period of Israel's history. It reflects the effort to create a new basis for understanding the world in the face of major shifts in the structures of society and in what was understood to be the logic of history. The earlier centers of the society in the court, the temple, and related economic institutions began to encounter competition in the new centers of the household and the school. In the latter setting, in particular, sages drew on their imaginations to envision a new world, different from the one presented by tradition, in order to prepare the young men who would be expected to bring that world into reality and to exercise leadership in it. These elite origins explain what is at heart a conservative thrust to the ethical views of wisdom literature. The new reality envisioned is one that will still allow those with experience, or at least a collective memory, of dominance to resume such positions. Missing are the calls for a redress of social inequities or the leveling of hierarchical structures that characterize much of the prophetic literature.

At the same time, wisdom literature affirms the persistent faithfulness of God that is known both in traditions of Israel's covenant relationships and in the beauty, bounty, and reliability of the creation. It is a theology in which lines between sacred and secular and between logic and piety alike are blurred. As a part of that integrative stance toward life and the world, wisdom literature expresses the assimilation into the people's theological self-understanding of symbols, traditions, and practices of the surrounding peoples with whom Israel's contact had increased during and after the exile. An important aspect of that assimilation includes the various goddess traditions, along with the theological models and mythic complexes that brought those traditions to expression in the mediation of the same God whose creative and redemptive involvement with the world was known to Israel through Torah, temple, and prophetic speech.[2]

Wisdom was an important term in that process of assimilation. As wisdom moved beyond the expression of conformity to the inner logic and coherence of God's creative presence, to express also God's active redemptive presence in the midst of the creation—and thus to symbolic expression in human form as the best we know of an active, willing agent—wisdom came to be personified as a woman.[3] This particular anthropomorphic category was reinforced both by echoes between what was confessed about wisdom and what was known about the divine functions carried by the goddesses of Israel's neighbors, and by the fact that in Hebrew (and, as would later be important, in Greek as well) the word for wisdom is grammatically feminine. Although grammatical and biological gender need not have any link, in this case it did, and Ms. Wisdom moved onto the stage, giving personality to an abstract concept. She is the personification of powers or realms of deity in a form that nevertheless protects Israelite monotheism. She is immanent to creation, yet distinct from it. She speaks in God's name, or one might even say that when Wisdom speaks, it is with God's voice. Contrary to the hypothesis of earlier Christian feminists who claimed that in Israelite religion and in Judaism the goddess was swallowed up by the male god YHWH, wisdom literature recognizes that the divine was worshiped in Israel in female as well as male forms.

Ms. Wisdom proves, however, to be an ambivalent icon of women's identity in divine form. That ambivalence has several dimensions. First, this personification is in a form recognized as female according to the canons of the kyriarchically assigned gender roles: She is a man's woman.[4] Her sphere of activity is principally the household and neighborhood, and her roles encompass primarily tasks of nurturing traditionally linked to women's activities. She breaks little new ground for women, especially in contrast to the expanded roles of many women in the society of postexilic Israel and Israel's diasporic communities. Second, Wisdom appears as ambivalent about her involvement with humankind. At one moment she hides herself, and at another she is said to seek out people to follow the "way" that she would teach them. Erotic language expresses people's—principally men's—longing for her and their desire to be found by her, such that her religious presence is veiled by her image as a sexual playmate. Finally, traditions that equate Wisdom with Torah, and thus sacrifice personality for permanence, or traditions that remove Wisdom from the role of mediator between creator and creation by confining her to the heavenly sphere, reflect a desire on the part of spokespersons for the official theology to limit or control Wisdom—to keep her in her place.

The literature is striking, however, in its affirmation of Wisdom's persistence in maintaining a corner of the religious imagination of the formative period common to both Judaism and Christianity. Exactly where Wisdom was venerated (whether in public or in private) is less clear—perhaps among some intellectual, cosmopolitan elites like those among whom the literature initially took shape, or perhaps among groups of women or others left on the margins of official religious practice focused on the Second Temple. Nevertheless, the words of Wisdom's life echo through that period—language of quest and longing, of light and way, of food and water, of word and life.[5]

WISDOM IN THE HEBREW BIBLE: FROM PRINCIPLE TO PRESENCE

Within the Hebrew Bible three texts introduce the term "wisdom" to identify the conformity of the creation to the will and even the nature of the Creator. That principle of the creation that begins as the focus of a hymn of praise in Psalm 104 becomes the object of humankind's most urgent quest according to Job 28. The author affirms, however, that the creation that itself embodies wisdom cannot reveal it. Rather it is revealed (Job 28:28) in an appropriate relationship to God, identified as יִרְאַת אֲדֹנָי or θεοσέβεια, often translated as "fear of God"—a construction conveying a sense of awe, reverence, respect, and piety. Already there wisdom moves toward being the self-revelation of God, and that movement is carried further in the opening chapters of Proverbs, where wisdom appears as an active presence, personified in female form, by which the divine nature and will are conveyed into the very midst of creation and of the human social order. Wisdom there expresses not merely God's self-disclosure, but God's active quest for relationship with humankind.

Psalm 104 (LXX 103)

Psalm 104 celebrates the beauty, order, stability, and grandeur of creation and attributes all of those qualities to the will and nature of the Creator.[6] Chaos is hemmed in (104:5–9), and at the same time creation's bounty overflows to the benefit of all life (104:10–18). Everything fits together in a reliable harmony that by implication provides a firm basis for human social life as well as for the rest of the creation, as can be seen in the inclusion of human labor as a part of the appropriate rhythm of the created order (Ps. 104:23) and not as punishment or curse (as in Gen. 3:17–19).

The psalmist concludes the celebration of creation (104:1–23) with "three telling conclusions"[7] (104:24–26, 27–30, and 31–34) and a pointed reminder that the gift of God's bounty nevertheless comes with a required response and consequences for its violation (v. 35). Of the three conclusions, the final one expresses the personal delight as well as wonder and awe of the psalmist. The second—almost in the form of a table grace—celebrates the daily dependence of creation on the Creator's continuing presence and care. It is the first of the conclusions that introduces language of "wisdom" (σοφία, חכמה — 104:24) as the guiding principle of all the "manifold works" of God. It is the source not only of the creative energy required to bring forth the bounty of the land and the waters of the earth, but also of the authority to transform the sea and its resident monsters from their usual role as symbols of impending chaos into a playground that is home to a frolicking pet (104:26). Even the warning carried by the final verse assumes a reliable universe in which the guilty will pay a price for their sin and, implicitly, the righteous will continue to enjoy the bounty of God's gifts.

Assigning a date to individual psalms is virtually impossible. The most that can be said about Psalm 104 is that it reflects a world view of relative optimism and security: God's bountiful creation is reliable, and, by implication, human life in harmony with that order can be expected to share in the bounty. The world works well, and the psalmist and those about whom he cares are able to take advantage of that good order. This suggests a time of prosperity, perhaps at the height of the Davidic monarchy, when such poetry would have found a home in the royal court, and a ready affirmation of its prayer to sustain and not to change the good order of God's creation.

Job 28

The saga of Job's sufferings and his debates with his alleged friends reflect a time when that reliable world was breaking down. Coming most likely from the sixth century B.C.E., Job reflects the chastening of the exile. No longer is the social order—and by implication even the creation itself—sure to provide blessings to those who live exemplary lives, as Job's own experience makes clear. Evidence of his suffering notwithstanding, he will not admit to the sin that his friends assume must be at its root: He has lived a righteous life, and a just God and a reliable world ought to bring him blessings. Chapter 28 comes in the midst of Job's lament in which he longs for the good old days (29:2), when his integrity meant something more tangible than his own sense of righteousness (27:2–6). The poem that constitutes chapter 28 represents one step in the discernment of a new understanding of God's ways as inaccessible to human intelligence and available only as a gift or revelation of the divine wisdom that is the foundation of the created order.

The four strophes of this hymn[8] describe the relentless, even violent, determination of human beings to wrest the secrets of God's design and plan for the creation from their deeply hidden places within that creation. Despite the wealth and secrets of the earth uncovered by their probing of its contours, wisdom still eludes their search (28:1–6, 7–12), and the commercial value of the earth's minerals and other riches does not begin to equal the value of wisdom to humankind (28:13–20). In fact, people's efforts to acquire wisdom by human effort amount to an attempt to become like God—an attempt as idolatrous as it is vain. Only rumors of wisdom echo in human knowing, and God alone perceives wisdom's way and knows wisdom's place, just as God alone has shaped the beauty and bounty of the creation and the ordinances that regulate it (28:21–28). God is craftsperson and judge of all that is, and wisdom is found in piety and obedience to God.

Similar to the role of wisdom in Psalm 104, wisdom in this hymn appears as the underlying principle of God's gracious and generous crafting of the world. Not a mediator or power, or even a collaborator with God in the creative enterprise, wisdom is seen, declared, established, and searched out by God. In this poem wisdom is not human understanding of the created order that results in knowledge of God, as many sages of the ancient world believed. Rather, wisdom must be revealed by God (28:23–28). Inaccessible to human intelligence or effort, wisdom comes to expression in a person's relationship with God that, in turn, gives shape to their understanding and behavior: "Indeed, it is the awe of God that is wisdom; and to depart from evil is understanding" (28:28; author's translation).[9]

The catch is that Job 1:1 describes Job as meeting precisely these criteria: He worships God and has shunned evil, and still he suffers! One waits in vain for Job to discover wisdom by another path,[10] and to discern another logic by which creation truly hangs together. If truth be told, however, the book resolves Job's dilemma by his restitution as the more or less benevolent patriarch of his household in a familiar world of order and dependability. That world, and not the view from his experiences of suffering, sets the framework for Job's final word on wisdom as the structure that still sustains the lamented good old days of his life and theology. Like many of the elites who looked to the return from exile through their memories of a time when they enjoyed at least a measure of power and prestige, Job too is able to reconstruct a good life for himself and his immediate family.

Proverbs 1–9

The other locus of wisdom references in the Hebrew Bible is in the book of Proverbs. The book as a whole consists of several discrete sections, each of which itself is a rather loose collection of related material. The figure of personified Wisdom is found in the first collection (1:1–9:18), which is identified in 1:1 as "The proverbs of Solomon son of David, king of Israel." This group of sayings linked by short essays contains material from different historical periods, but its redaction in its present form is clearly postexilic, probably from the late sixth or early fifth century. Concerns about land distribution (and attendant economic stratification); family structure as the center of political, economic, and sacred life; and pressures from foreign influences on the religion and society of Israel reflect that time of return. At that time the crisis of the exile was still a fresh memory, and the later postexilic focus on Torah as the key to structuring the community's life was not yet as sharp as it would subsequently become.

That social context supported a dramatic increase in the power and authority belonging to women who managed the households and were crucial links in the transmission of the religious traditions and practices of the community that centered in the home and family. The models for the ideal woman described in Proverbs (in Prov. 31, for example) can be found in these powerful women of the postexilic community who were so essential to its survival and prosperity. These same actual women may also have shaped the personified figure of Wisdom, thus both connecting and reshaping Jewish monotheism through the life experiences and contextual realities of women.[11]

Carol A. Newsom and Athalya Brenner[12] debate the particular literary devices by which the author has reflected, or reflected on, this situation of women's prominence. Both recognize that the overt design of Proverbs 1–9 takes the form of a father's instructions to a son. Brenner argues on the basis of parallels in other literature of the period that one should consider the narrator as an overriding "F" voice enveloping those two "M" voices, like a mother encouraging her children to listen to their father (4:1) and thus functioning as the actually superior power, albeit working, as it were, behind the throne. It is the very invisibility of this "F" voice that makes it hard to see how that voice prevails over those of the more solid "M" characters.

Newsom, on the other hand, finds the issue at stake in these chapters to be the formation of the subjectivity of the reader. She concludes that in fact the literary devices reinforce the patriarchal values of the culture. The setting is a family, which, because everyone has or had one, gives the false appearance of ideological innocence. Nevertheless, given the prominence of the family as social unit in the postexilic period, in this literature family roles carry the sustaining values of the culture into subsequent generations. The male identity of the principal characters implies that readers should identify with the son whose goal is to appropriate the father's teaching and eventually the father's place in the family. A central theme of the teaching is precisely that the child must resist any rival discourse to that of the father. The speeches of personified Wisdom reinforce that central discourse, and, despite the female character, "belong to the same cultural voice,"[13] as is seen through her complementary authoritative position. Hers is the public authoritative voice corresponding to the father's voice in the family.

Rival discourses come from an unidentified man linked to the inversion of values against which the son is warned (2:12–14). The epitome of otherness, however, is found in the "strange" or "foreign" woman encountered at various points through Proverbs 1–9. According to Newsom, "She is the contradiction, the dissonance that forces a dominant discourse to articulate itself and at the same time threatens to subvert it."[14] She does not speak for herself. Instead she is met in the father's warnings—a woman talked about as an object of male discourse. Her threat to the practical and symbolic order is thus managed.

Wisdom, however, is a female character—a subject who is an "other" to the dominant discourse—who nevertheless speaks on her own behalf. That very fact plants in her speech the seeds of crisis in both the practical and the symbolic order. Her threat is contained by her authoritative articulations of the central value of that order, wisdom itself. Her speech of self-disclosure, paired with the portrait of her opposite, serves to "define and secure the boundaries of the symbolic order of patriarchal wisdom."[15]

Contrary to the occurrences of wisdom in Psalms and Job, wisdom in Proverbs has clearly moved beyond a principle reflected in the order, bounty, and reliability of the creation, or even a hypostasis or the representation of a trait or quality of God, to a personification of a religious symbol that expresses the human experience of the transcendent. Although parts of the description of Wisdom echo the self-praise of various goddesses (including, in particular, the multiplicity of images applied to her, including counselor, lover, bride, erotic consort, mother, daughter, teacher, and administrator of divine justice), these images leave "little more than traces"[16] of any representation of a goddess. Instead, the personification of both wisdom and folly as literary characters in Proverbs functions pedagogically to recall people to the awe or "fear" of God that is the beginning of knowledge.

From the very outset, personified Wisdom and YHWH are represented as sharing common authority and responsibility, especially as the giver of life (see 1:17 and 1:20–33). In these early glimpses of Wisdom that open the parenthesis around the central didactic material (which will be closed by the Wisdom hymns of Proverbs 8 and 9), we meet Wisdom on the streets—a figure midway between a pleading parent and a scold—wanting to spare others from the consequences of their actions and yet warning them that her patience with their persistent turning from her ways is about to expire! She is the maker and indicator of the "way" (2:8–20), which is a social construct—a path through life worn by many feet, which over time becomes the preferred or even the only acceptable route by which to negotiate in an ethically appropriate manner the terrain of choices and behaviors. In 3:13–32 Wisdom is introduced as the desirable woman of every man's longing—dispenser of life, agent of wealth and honor, a pleasing companion to sustain one on life's course (see also 4:7–9). She is the opposite of the equally stereotypical "strange" woman—a symbol of disorder on all levels[17]—who is out to lure men away from faithfulness to their families, their society, and their God. Wisdom's precepts alone provide sound guidance for life in human community.

Wisdom's wise precepts are escalated in chapter 8 in hymns of self-praise. The chapter falls naturally into five parts. Proverbs 8:1–3 provides the sage's introduction to the figure of Wisdom and reflects the school setting of the work. Wisdom's call to humankind is set forth in 8:4–11, and it is paralleled in 8:32–36 by instructions exhorting people to embody the teaching that Wisdom represents. These sections frame two poems that celebrate Wisdom's providential rule (8:12–21) and Wisdom's place in creation (8:22–31). In the first of these poems, using language and images drawn from public and private realms alike, Wisdom dispenses to rulers the power of legitimate governance and the justice they need to rule. She grants to her lovers both life and wealth (8:12–21). The second poem describes the origin of the cosmos (8:22–26) and the place of wisdom in creation

(8:27–31). Perdue summarizes, "Drawing on important metaphors from cosmological and anthropological traditions, Proverbs 8 provokes the imagination to conceive of reality as the well-designed world of a divine architect who, by means of wisdom, proportions its components into a harmonious, elegant whole."[18]

The claims made about Wisdom and the form of the wisdom hymns themselves resemble Hellenistic praises of the goddess Isis and Egyptian celebrations of Maat. Such remnants of goddess language that refer to Wisdom in the midst of the overarching structure of monotheism lead naturally to the question of how this personified figure was understood to be related to YHWH: What understandings encompass the affirmation of her priority among all of creation and even recognize her as God's agent in the creation, and at the same time do not set her up as a divine competitor? Two dimensions of that question must be explored. First, one must address the question of how she came into existence; second, there is the question of how her power and authority are exercised.

At issue is whether Wisdom is part of the creation, or whether Wisdom existed prior to God's act of creation. This issue is crucial. If the latter is the case, Wisdom's subordination to God is less clear, and Wisdom becomes a power in her own right. The debate turns on the appropriate meaning of the Hebrew root קנה in Proverbs 8:22. Modern translations generally render it "create," making Wisdom the first of God's created artifacts. According to this interpretation, wisdom is the principle of logic undergirding the creation as a sort of prototype for God's subsequent work. As Bruce Vawter has argued through painstaking lexical study, however, such translations mask the word's more usual meaning of "get," "discover," or "acquire,"[19] in order to protect the theological assumption that only God existed prior to the creation, and all that is—Wisdom included—proceeded from God's creative work. On the contrary, the perspective of the author appears to be that God is not the creator of wisdom, but rather its discoverer.

Carole Fontaine escapes the literalism of the alternative posed by this problem of translation. She recognizes the tensive quality of the symbol of wisdom to identify in the text a picture of Wisdom (personified, in this case) both as "conceived" (8:22) and "brought forth" (8:24)—in other words, as a sexually conceived child of God—and as a preexistent entity whom YHWH acquires as a first step in the creation. God then builds Wisdom's own design into the ordering of the universe that God and Wisdom will carry out together. Even early Greek translations of Proverbs reflect the theological struggle inherent in the Hebrew root, with the LXX using the verb κτίζω, "create," while other Greek translations of Proverbs 8:22 used κτάομαι, "procure," "acquire," or "get"—a word that the LXX uses to translate קנה elsewhere. In later translations Wisdom then becomes the "model" of God's works, as ראשית דרכו should probably be understood.

Related to the question of Wisdom's origins is that of Wisdom's role. Wisdom and God are portrayed as craftspeople in the same studio. Wisdom is also the homemaker—maker of the house and manager of the estate—a role at the heart of the life of the society of postexilic Israel. Wisdom is nurturer and provider, host of a bountiful table (9:5),[20] and someone who summons people to a mature way (9:6)—two roles proper to the God of the exodus traditions. Wisdom's commands and indictments echo the prophetic oracles bearing a word directly from YHWH, and the authority of Wisdom's voice likewise echoes that of YHWH (1:20–23). Like YHWH, Wisdom is giver of life (1:33), one to whom the people cry (1:28), and the authority by whom monarchs rule (8:15–16). Clearly Wisdom has moved beyond mere representation of divine powers to function as a symbol expressing humankind's experience of God as creator, giver of life, judge, and provider: In these roles she takes over the work of God.[21]

As a reality accessible to God, Wisdom stands outside of God as the autonomy of order, justice, and reason in the universe. In that sense, Wisdom is partner and shaper of God's work, as much as God is of Wisdom's. Wisdom and YHWH work in partnership, or more properly, in interdependence. With all of this, how can Wisdom not be seen as an independent deity and thus a threat to Israel's monotheism? And if Wisdom is not an independent deity, how is Wisdom's role in both the creative and the redemptive work of God to be understood? A way through this theological conundrum can be found in 8:30–31: Wisdom is God's delight, and Wisdom, in turn, delights in humankind. Wisdom thus functions as the "primary link" between God and humankind,[22] or, more properly, as the way God is actively present in the world. Through Wisdom, the movement happens in both directions: The desire of Wisdom for intimacy with humankind becomes the vehicle for divine presence on earth, and at the same time humankind's desire for Wisdom draws humankind toward God.[23]

WISDOM IN THE DEUTEROCANONICAL LITERATURE: A JEWISH LEGACY IN THE HELLENISTIC WORLD

During the period when the books were written that appear as deuterocanonical books in the Christian canon, Judaism was addressing questions of identity and lifestyle in the context of pressures toward enculturation in the Hellenistic world. Texts focusing on Wisdom proved an important challenge in that task. On the one hand, they provided a bridge of common language with other religious and philosophical movements of the surrounding culture. On the other hand, that very common language and imagery had to be linked to the centers of Jewish identity in Torah and in the continuing saga of Jewish history if these texts were to avoid so thorough an assimilation that they jeopardized precisely the expression of Jewish identity that was their purpose. Sirach, Baruch, and the Wisdom of Solomon represent three distinct approaches to that task.

Sirach[24]

The writer of Sirach appears as a scribe in charge of a school for young men from Jerusalem's upper class in the early second century B.C.E. The education they received prepared them to succeed in the increasingly complex and cosmopolitan Hellenistic world. The aristocratic male audience of the book can be discerned in the intricate interweaving of sexual and economic issues as factors in male honor, to which those seeking wisdom must be attentive. In both arenas the longing for the external signs of control and stability so elusive in that confusing and volatile context would come into sharp focus. Much of this book, which was originally written in Hebrew,[25] echoes the book of Proverbs in identifying personified Wisdom as a teacher about right and wrong ways of living, on whom the righteous person delights to meditate (4:11; 14:20–27). Wisdom as a principle is equated with awe or "fear" of God (1:11–30) and obedience to Torah (15:1). Service to wisdom is also service to "the Holy One," and it is the route to many blessings, while abandonment of wisdom is the road to ruin (4:11–19; 6:18–31). Sirach, however, does not simply echo the common logic that would see a direct link between good behavior and good fortune. Essential to his new construction is his reappropriation of the Wisdom myth found already in Proverbs, in correlation with the social order of Second Temple Judaism and with the narrative of Israel's history. Sapiential forms and conventions are linked to sacred narrative.[26]

The book begins with a hymn portraying wisdom as a creation of the Creator (1:1–10), thus echoing earlier affirmations in Job 28 and elsewhere of "a basic correlation between the world and the human capacity for understanding it, anchored in divine intention and activity."[27] Wisdom is universal and accessible to all. At the beginning of the second half of the book, however, in the hymn of Sirach 24, the picture changes. Here, in many ways like the hymns of and to Wisdom in Proverbs 1–9, Wisdom now sings her own praises from a heavenly stage and describes her wanderings through creation in search of a home. Is "she" a goddess in her own right who praises her virtues and powers?[28] Not really, for despite the divine origins and cosmic rule claimed by Wisdom, she functions as God's agent, and she ends the quest for an earthly home in the place and among the people of God's choosing.

Following a brief introit, the hymn unfolds in six strophes. The first (24:3–6) posits Wisdom in the role of the divine speech that calls forth the creation in Genesis 1. Wisdom's presence in the "pillar of cloud" evokes the story of God's abiding with Israel in Numbers 33:7–11. Wisdom's restless dominion over all creation described in the first strophe leads to Wisdom's home being established—neither by Wisdom's own choice, nor because of human merit, but by God's decree—in Israel, and specifically in the tabernacle in Zion (strophe 2; 24:7–11). The creation outlined in the first strophe is recast to place Wisdom also as a part of the creation fashioned by God. Furthermore, by God's design, Israel's history and the pilgrimage of Wisdom are joined. Wisdom is not merely a stand-in for the plot line of God's history with Israel, however, but is also depicted in the third strophe (24:12–17) as taking the form of lush vegetation. From agent of creation, Wisdom has taken root, as it were, in the finished product. From this fixed place, Wisdom becomes the tree of life that provides nourishment—a continuous flow between hunger and fulfillment—for the people God has chosen (strophe 4; 24:19–22), offering her fruit to those who hunger and thirst.

Strophe 5 (24:23–29) represents the principal innovation of this Wisdom poem, in which Wisdom is identified with Torah, "the Book of the Covenant of God Most High." This localization of Wisdom allows Sirach to avoid the skepticism of Job 28, where it is uncertain whether wisdom will be found, but to do so by a nationalist focus that is echoed in Baruch 3:9–4:4. The Law itself is sufficient to make wisdom abound, though only as God's gift and not as the achievement of human intelligence. As Torah, Wisdom is the source of life. In strophe 6 (24:30–34) water of life replaces the tree of life as the image by which this life-giving property is conveyed. Unlike the tree that remains where it is planted, the water moves out to cover vast reaches of the creation with the "discipline" and "teaching" that convey life, just as in the first strophe Wisdom traveled with majestic strides over the whole universe.

As Torah, Wisdom becomes a lasting symbol of God's will and presence and is identified with the most sacred expression of Israel's relationship with God. The work of the scribe, then, is to convey both the depths of wisdom and the specificity of Torah to the people on whom God has chosen to bestow both. Wisdom's song joins the drama of salvation, in the form of a fixed deposit of teaching deemed to convey the authoritative voice of God and to make clear the choice between the way of life and the way of death.[29]

Whether the identity with Torah represents a step forward or backward in Wisdom's life as a symbol and focus of the faith and religious life of the people is a moot point. Confined to the limits of Torah—narrative and law—Wisdom is clearly under God's control, with no activity or personality, despite her continuing ability to mediate life to others. Like the women of Sirach's own society, Wisdom herself required control and limitation as part of the project to reinscribe a stable social and religious order. Such a reconstructed and well-ordered world would guarantee the place of those elites whom scribes like Sirach served. In exchange, Wisdom received the gift of transformation into the durability of a text and its power to mediate stability in a time of social and religious chaos.[30]

Baruch 3:9–4:4

The book of Baruch, produced most likely in the late second or early first century B.C.E.,[31] follows Job, Proverbs, and Sirach in recognizing that wisdom is hidden from humanity. The book itself is attributed to Baruch, secretary to Jeremiah, and allegedly written to the exiled king "Jeconiah" (really Jehoiachin) in the fifth year after the fall of Jerusalem (587/6 B.C.E.). Although its real date is considerably later, the issue of exile—how and why had this happened, and how might a recurrence be prevented?—gives the book in general, and the hymn to Wisdom in particular, its shape and theological focus. The language and imagery of the hymn in 3:9–4:4 draw on the earlier pictures of wisdom in Proverbs, Job, and Ben Sira. Inaccessible to human efforts at understanding despite its presence throughout the creation (see Job 28), wisdom comes only as the gift of God to Israel. That gift is embodied especially in the precepts of Torah (see also Sir. 24:23–29), which Israelites must heed if they are to "return" from their exile and find new life as a people (3:9, 37; 4:1–4). Wisdom known and heeded in those precepts becomes the source of strength, understanding, light, peace, and life itself (3:13–14). The explicit nationalism of this poem contrasts with the more cosmopolitan view of Job but supports the perspective of Sirach 24. The personification of wisdom is less clear in the hymn in Baruch than in Sirach 24, however, in that the former is *about* wisdom, while in the latter it is Wisdom who speaks.[32]

Wisdom of Solomon

Written in Greek somewhere between the last half of the first century B.C.E. and the beginning of the Common Era, the Wisdom of Solomon[33] is probably the latest Jewish writing in the Greek canon of Jewish scriptures. It reflects the philosophical concerns and cultural stress of Israel's life in the Diaspora, especially in Alexandria, Egypt. Claiming to represent the wisdom of the great King Solomon, the author rails against a lifestyle of sensual gratification (1:16–2:24) and the worship of idols (13:1–15:17), which together threaten to attract Jews away from the monotheism at the heart of Jewish religion and toward the syncretism of the Hellenistic environment. Silvia Schroer attributes the warnings of Wisdom of Solomon 1–5[34] to the last third of the first century B.C.E., when there was already some lapse of practice among Alexandrian Jews, and even some persecution of Jews by Jews. She attributes Wisdom of Solomon 6–9 to the period after Octavian seized power over Egypt in 30 B.C.E., when the impact of the Pax Romana came to be felt there. The book's reminder of the humanity and mortality of kings stood in contrast to the claims of Rome, and also to the criteria of enduring rulership in personified Wisdom and in Solomon, the ideal (and idealized) wise king. Finally, Wisdom of Solomon 10–19—a hymnic retelling of Israel's history, with special emphasis on the account of the people's deliverance from an earlier oppressive regime in Egypt—reflects a period of rising anti-Semitism in Egypt, and the Jewish people's corresponding visions of national liberation. Such an ethos fits well with the middle of the reign of Augustus, just prior to the common era.[35]

The author's premise is that the pursuit of wisdom, coupled with a righteous life, is the sole route to the immortality that is the aim of all religion. The author's resulting argument is a complex balance of rejecting Hellenistic thought and literary expressions, all the while using them in the defense of the integrity and superiority of the Jewish religion. The author appears to have in mind a multifaceted audience, including Jews struggling to remain rooted in their ancestral religion; Jews who have already compromised with the religious and philosophical environment in which they are living; and Gentiles who might be persuaded to embrace Judaism, or at the very least to back away from anti-Semitic attitudes and behavior. The result of the author's complex agenda is an expression of Hellenized Judaism in which common human goals related to the pursuit of wise conduct are connected to Jewish religious practice, and in which Wisdom's permeation and ordering of the entire cosmos are linked to Israel's own story of divine election and redemption.

The three sections (or "books") that correspond to the three occasions identified by Schroer can be called the book of eschatology (1:9–5:23 or 6:11); the book of wisdom (6:1 or 6:12–9:18); and the book of history (10:1–19:22). All three parts reflect on wisdom, righteousness and sin, and immortality and death. The opening affirmation sets the stage: Wisdom, equated with God's spirit, is the cosmic force holding together all creation including human history and social institutions and dwelling in individual persons as God's self-manifestation to all who seek God (1:1–8). The "book of eschatology" then contrasts right and wrong perceptions of how salvation is attained for the individual and how human society is ordered to reflect the meaning crafted by God into the creation itself. The search for wisdom that the author recommends is corroborated in Solomon's own quest, which, in turn, is intertwined with the description of wisdom in the second "book," in which the eschatological gift of immortality is already conveyed to the righteous through the indwelling presence of wisdom.[36] Finally, the "book of history" celebrates the conformity of Israel's own story to wisdom's logic—a particular though not necessarily exclusive embodiment of wisdom in human history. Wisdom takes on the divine role of redeemer, both of individual righteous souls and of the people of God's election, as wisdom's salvific power becomes the basis for reinterpreting Israel's saving history.[37]

In the "book of wisdom" (6:12–9:18), Solomon's quest alternates with descriptions of wisdom's characteristics and gifts, both as a personified figure and with the background of such common meanings of wisdom as study, knowledge, experience, and cleverness in the background (6:9, 11, 25). What to call wisdom is an increasingly complex problem as the description in Wisdom of Solomon unfolds. Designations such as "hypostasis" or "divine attribute" or metaphorical personification of cosmic order fail to do justice to the vitality and initiative of wisdom as an expression of the divine, "a manifestation of God to human beings."[38] The twenty-one epithets (three times the perfect number seven) applied to Wisdom in 7:22–8:1 make clear the impossibility of adequately describing Wisdom, and at the same time they escalate the discourse on Wisdom to parallel hymns and treatises in which deities from Egypt, Greece, and other cultures are praised in many names and forms.[39] Elusive as Wisdom is, however, unlike the mysteries, Wisdom is accessible to humankind as an ethical preceptor—teacher of both wisdom and righteousness: "Righteousness and wisdom are like the outer and inner sides of a life pleasing to God. Without wisdom, there can be no just 'reign of God.' "[40]

Divine speech (as in Genesis 1) and wisdom are equated in the act of creation (9:1–2). Wisdom is the glory of God (7:25–26), the mediator of creation (8:5–6), and companion at the throne of God (9:10). Wisdom is the renewer of creation, powerful beyond earthly rulers, and present throughout all that is. Wisdom's ability to permeate all things (7:22b–8:1) speaks of divine immanence without merging God into the creation itself.[41] Wisdom is, in Elisabeth Schüssler Fiorenza's words,

> . . . an initiate into the knowledge of G*d, collaborator in G*d's work, the brightness that streams from everlasting light, a pure effervescence of divine glory, the image of G*d's goodness. In short, Divine Wisdom lives symbiotically with G*d (Wisd. 8:3f.; 7:26). Kinship with Wisdom brings immortality and friendship with her, resulting in pure delight (Wisd. 10:17).[42]

In Wisdom reside knowledge, authority, counsel, rule, teaching, and the power to form and create. Wisdom is God's gift that, in turn, brings other gifts—an artisan in shaping the cosmos who can then teach its ways to human beings who are equally the products of Wisdom's formation.[43]

Wisdom thus emerges in the Second Temple period as a powerful and persuasive religious symbol in those roles as a feminine figure, despite the overarching male dominance of that period. Wisdom is one with God (7:25–26), distinguishable but inseparable—the involvement of the divine in the world. Here, as in Proverbs 1–9 and Sirach, the relationship between Wisdom and the various goddess cults of Israel's neighbors is open to debate. Clearly some of the terms by which Wisdom is portrayed as the lover and even royal consort and co-regent with YHWH echo portraits of Isis, Maat, and other Egyptian and Syrian goddesses. How the obvious syncretism would have been understood, however, is not clear. No longer is Wisdom merely the personification of divine order or creativity, or a hypostasis of a male God, but neither is Wisdom a competitor with YHWH as the one deity who is the author of life. To some people, Wisdom may have represented a threat to be contained, but to many Wisdom was the key to life, and life eternal. In Wisdom the yearning for independence and the unquenchable nationalism of Israel came together with universalism and deliberate enculturation. They came together in this symbol critical of all governing powers that fell short of the divine justice with which Wisdom was frequently linked. In addition, Wisdom showed the way to a "just Jewish life amid a pluralistic world," and thus stood as "an authentic biblical image of God."[44] Whether Wisdom was actually worshiped as an independent expression of the deity is unknown, but the close resemblance between qualities and actions ascribed to Wisdom and those ascribed to YHWH make it seem likely that Wisdom had become for many the focus of Jewish devotion and piety, and a "way" to the very heart of God.

CIRCUMSCRIBED WISDOM IN
1 ENOCH, 2 ESDRAS, AND PHILO

In both the biblical and the deuterocanonical books, wisdom expresses God's presence and self-disclosure in the created order. Wisdom is thus a mediating figure, one that assures that divine transcendence does not mean divine absence. While it is tempting to move immediately from that affirmation to an examination of the role of wisdom in the Fourth Gospel, which seems in many ways to continue that tradition, another current must first be explored. That current is represented in brief passages in *1 Enoch* and *2 Esdras* and in the writings of Philo. Wisdom's mediating role is abridged in both cases by Wisdom's relegation to heaven, having abandoned the quest for a suitable earthly dwelling place. The influence of platonic dualism further compels Philo to minimize the female imagery so powerfully present elsewhere in the wisdom traditions, including the assumption of many roles assigned elsewhere to the grammatically feminine σοφία by the grammatically masculine λόγος. The introduction of the latter term, however, especially in intimate connection with wisdom traditions, introduces an additional significant ingredient in the background to the presence of wisdom in the Fourth Gospel.

1 Enoch 41:1–2; 2 Esdras 5:9b–10a

In the apocalyptic writings of *1 Enoch* and *2 Esdras* (both most likely from the end of the Second Temple period), personified Wisdom gives up completely on finding a dwelling place on earth. In what looks like a parody on Sirach 24 and Baruch 3:9–4:4, the unrighteousness of Israel has driven Wisdom back to heaven. Jerusalem cannot contain her, nor can the Torah given to Israel provide her a toehold among humankind. Instead, what before was represented as her powerful divine presence on earth is elevated into heavenly absence and to the company of the angels. She is safely limited not in any loss of personal agency but in access by those human beings whose faith takes shape around her.

Philo

The limitation of σοφία is even harsher in the writings of the first-century Alexandrian philosopher Philo.[45] In the logic of his system of thought, the affirmation of Jewish monotheism acquires symbolic expression in an androcentric gender dualism that reflects a philosophical anthropology similar to that of Plato and Aristotle. According to this system of meaning, all that is heavenly, spiritual, intellectual, eternal, and perfect is expressed in masculine language and male symbols, while all that is transient, imperfect, physical, and earthly is represented in feminine language and female symbols. This point of view is expressed in a generally negative view of women, with the exception of the monastic community of the Therapeutrides, who, in their quest for wisdom, have remained childless and even virgins—in other words, as close to "male" as women can get.[46]

Not surprisingly, Philo's portrait of Wisdom goes hand in hand with his negative portrayal of femaleness in relationship to the divine. His project has two phases. First, Wisdom's gender is interpreted theologically. As female, she is subordinate to God, just as all virtues—by grammar feminine and by mythological depiction female—occupy a place subordinate to "the one who makes all things": The masculine always has preeminence, and the feminine is always found wanting. Wisdom is called "daughter of God," and she is said to have no mother (*Questions and Answers on Genesis* 4.145). She is described as a perpetual virgin whose purity and divine paternity allow her to remain undefiled. As a result, this eldest child, "daughter of God," is also a father: "The name of Wisdom is female, but her nature male," and thus she or he is able to provide instruction and guide people in disciplined learning (*On Flight and Finding* 50–52). The λόγος, in turn, is the "son of God" (*On Husbandry* 51–52), and thus God's eldest masculine offspring (*On Flight and Finding* 101–2; *On the Change of Names* 15).

In the second phase of Philo's reinterpretation, Wisdom is the mother of creation as well as of the λόγος (*On Flight and Finding* 109; *Questions and Answers on Genesis* 4.97), but she is identified with the upper realms of the divine and is no longer found going to and fro on earth, seeking those who will receive her. Instead, only her "representation and copy" in the form of the tabernacle marks her static place on earth (*Heir of Divine Things* 112). At the same time the word, or λόγος—grammatically masculine, and thus easily linked symbolically with such male figures as the High Priest—replaces her in the soteriological role as guide on the way that mediates salvation (*On Flight and Finding* 109–10), as well as in her traditional mediating function, representing God as active in the world of sense perception (*On Flight and Finding* 108–10; *On Dreams* 2.242).

CONCLUSION

These various wisdom texts and traditions link wisdom to God's role as creator and to God's life-giving and redemptive power. On the one hand, wisdom is the content of what one must know to understand the deep logic underlying the natural world and the social order alike. That logic transcends the disorder of even the most tumultuous events and historical moments and thus gives shape to lives and communities uprooted by public or personal trauma. By discerning that coherence (be it through God's gift or human effort) and by following the ethical "way" consistent with it, people could shape their lives in congruence with God's will. On the other hand, more than simply the content of God's creative acts, Wisdom is also God's working partner, or perhaps even the expression of God's own creative self. As the self-disclosure of Wisdom, then, creation is not simply something God has done, but a glimpse into the very heart and nature of God.

The figure of Wisdom also unites God's work as creator at the beginning of time with God's passion for continued and, where necessary, restored relationship with humankind. The discernment of wisdom and the ethical choice to follow wisdom's way remain elusive, and hence the portrait of Wisdom wandering the streets of the city seeking people who will follow her way expresses the divine commitment to continue to accompany God's people and to mediate to them life in its fullness, regardless of human failures. Wisdom lives in the symbols of bread, water, and wine that bless and sustain physical life and point toward the essence of life not limited by human finitude. Wisdom is not easily put off by people's failure to welcome her, but rather she continues to seek them out in the face of rejection and of their turning from the way she has taught. In other words, Wisdom's relentless faithfulness expresses God's identity as redeemer and sustainer as well as creator.

The hymns that tell the story of Wisdom sing a melody of hope and promise that has resonated with Jews of every age in their quest to live out their covenant obligations with God. Those hymns and related traditions appear to have been particularly powerful for people living in various periods of historical chaos. They took shape and developed throughout the Second Temple period, particularly in the stress of the political and economic domination, cultural diversity, and religious pluralism of the Diaspora. The poets who crafted the hymns adopted and adapted elements of that diversity to enrich and interpret the fundamental tenets of their religion: worship of God alone, and life normed by God's will mediated by Torah and the way of Wisdom. For communities like that of the Fourth Gospel, these same wisdom traditions gave expression to their own confidence in God's persistent faithfulness and redemptive presence known now in Jesus Christ.

While what was affirmed about Wisdom's power and way may have given voice to many of the Christians' affirmations about Jesus, her feminine personification surely collided with Jesus' male identity. At this point, Philo's introduction of the λόγος as bearing both a cosmological and a salvific role connected to and in some sense replacing that of Wisdom establishes Philo as a significant bridge figure between the earlier wisdom texts and the Fourth Gospel.[47] In that Gospel the programmatic hymn (John 1:1–18) celebrates the λόγος in terms reminiscent of the wisdom hymns of Proverbs, Sirach, and the Wisdom of Solomon, and it sets the stage for the amplification of wisdom motifs throughout the Gospel. That grammatically masculine word, with its attendant masculine pronouns, establishes the link between wisdom motifs and the man Jesus in whom "the λόγος became flesh."

Chapter 4

Wisdom Made Flesh

None of the biblical or deuterocanonical texts that describe Wisdom is quoted in the Fourth Gospel. Add to that fact the absence of the word σοφία from this Gospel, and one might wonder whether the Fourth Gospel can be linked to the motifs of wisdom at all. The closest the Fourth Gospel comes to a passage that speaks of divine Wisdom is the hymn of John 1:1–18, which speaks not of "wisdom," but of "the word" (ὁ λόγος). The two-pronged question that this evidence evokes, then, is can we even speak of "wisdom theology (or Christology)" or a "wisdom hymn" in the Fourth Gospel? If so, how are we to understand the significance of that agenda in this Gospel?

One conclusion that might be reached, of course, is that the author of the Gospel simply used a poem or hymn about the λόγος known in the Johannine community in order to make some christological claims about Jesus, without deliberately invoking wisdom traditions or wisdom theology at all. In keeping with that suggestion, the author would simply have incorporated this isolated hymn for its intrinsic imagery as an introduction to the Gospel. The evidence assembled in this chapter corroborates the consensus among Johannine interpreters that this should indeed be seen as a "wisdom hymn," and in fact that it connects to the motifs found in a number of the wisdom texts considered in the previous chapter. This evidence suggests, further, that allusions to divine Wisdom and Wisdom's roles are present much more pervasively in the Fourth Gospel than in just a poetic "prologue" or introductory artistic flourish.

Wisdom theology may indeed have been in the author's mind, but known through the lens of such cultural influences as Philo's argument that ὁ λόγος is the appropriate replacement for Wisdom as a personification of divine presence on earth, while Wisdom remains safe in the heavenly regions. Since the Fourth Gospel nowhere replicates his argument for that change of vocabulary, however, it seems inappropriate to attribute to the author direct or deliberate dependence on Philo's work. The hymn may then simply have existed in its present form, conveniently at hand among the resources expressing wisdom theology in the author's cultural environment. The author might also have crafted this poem drawing on images of the λόγος as a synonym of divine Wisdom, simply because that was the most familiar language by which those traditions could be conveyed. After all, such texts as Sirach 24:3 and Wisdom of Solomon 9:1–2 also posit a parallelism between Wisdom as an agent in the creation and God's creative word or speech. Given the significance of God's "word" or speech (דבר) elsewhere in the Hebrew Bible, that might simply have seemed to the author like an appropriate way to invoke both the wisdom traditions explicitly and other dimensions of the biblical heritage at the same time.

Another possible explanation of the λόγος language of this hymn, of course, is that the author deliberately invoked the content of traditions about divine Wisdom and deliberately made the change from the grammatically feminine word σοφία to the grammatically masculine word λόγος. Such a change might have been prompted by a determination to eclipse language pointing toward feminine imagery for God, or to avoid the paradox of portraying the male Jesus as the incarnation of a feminine expression of God that the tradition spoke of as in fact a female.[1] While final resolution of such questions is impossible, they will remain on the agenda as we examine the hymn in detail in the discussion that follows.

Despite the identification of John 1:1–18 as a "wisdom hymn" in almost every modern commentary, few authors take the additional step to argue for a substantive link in the remainder of the Gospel between Wisdom as a manifestation of the divine and Jesus as the λόγος incarnate.[2] Explanations for that silence fall usually into one of two categories. First, there is the accurate observation that after the hymn, ὁ λόγος is never again used explicitly as a christological title or designation of Jesus himself. The second set of arguments revolves around the hymn as the product of and insertion by a later redactor, and hence not part of the portrait of Jesus intended by the author of (most of) the rest of the Fourth Gospel. Conclusions about authorial intent are impossible both to prove and to disprove, however. Furthermore, while it is clear that the Gospel has undergone several editions (as can be seen in such evidence as the interruption of the farewell discourse in 14:31, the "premature" conclusion of the Gospel in 20:30–31, and the cycles of reflection on the meaning of the "bread of life" in 6:35–65), positing an early level as belonging to the author and a later one — which usually includes the opening hymn — as including additions by someone with another point of view seems speculative at best.

This study sidesteps that debate by working with the canonical form of the text as the creation of the one we call "the author" of what is clearly the product of a community's life and faith. That means beginning with the "wisdom hymn" to discern what in fact is said about this figure. Part of that discussion must entail reflection on the use of λόγος rather than σοφία to make the author's point, and identification of both parallels to the hymns to divine Wisdom known in the tradition and significant differences from those hymns. The rest of this chapter then follows two lines of argument. The first explores substantive links between the hymn and the rest of the Gospel. The second identifies other dimensions of Wisdom known in the tradition that also come to expression in the author's portrait of Jesus and of the community of his followers.

THE HYMN TO THE WORD
Structure and Literary Context

The Fourth Gospel begins with a hymn—or to be more precise, a poem with commentary—that celebrates Christ as the Word, ὁ λόγος. Few editions of the New Testament actually present John 1:1–18 in verse form, but the repetitions of language and the parallel rhythms of many pairs of lines make that designation easy to accept. Various commentators have proposed different ways of arranging the material, and while their arguments may be of significance to students of Greek poetic structure, for the purposes of this study, the proposal of Raymond Brown will suffice as an example.[3] He identifies four strophes with prose interpolations and a brief concluding statement. The first strophe, verses 1–2, establishes the existence of the λόγος in God's presence "in the beginning." The second, verses 3–5, sets forth the role of the λόγος in creating "all things," and in particular "life" (equated with "light"). The first prose interpolation (vv. 6–9) comes between the second and third strophes and introduces the "witness" of John the Baptist. The third strophe (vv. 10–12b) portrays the ambivalent results of the entry of the λόγος into the world. That strophe is followed by a brief amplification of the identification of those who did accept the λόγος (vv. 12c–13). The final strophe presents the incarnation of the λόγος (vv. 14, 16). This strophe again is interrupted and concluded with brief interpretative comments (vv. 15, 17–18), the latter of which mentions Jesus Christ for the first time.

Following the hymn, the tone shifts abruptly from poetry to "testimony," as the brief comment about John the Baptist in verses 6–9 is amplified with direct discourse in verses 19–28 and then demonstrated when his encounter with Jesus is described in verses 29–34. Christological designations pile up in John's testimony, in the transfer of his disciples to Jesus (vv. 35–42), and in the chain of testimonies as one disciple calls the next, until the community of followers has been formed and Jesus himself points forward to the "greater things" they will see (vv. 43–51). Although the narrative project of this section of the Gospel is the gathering of Jesus' disciples, it is clear that establishing the identity of the one to whom they come, and who "remains" with them (the verb μένω, which figures so prominently in establishing the motif of friendship, is introduced in this section), is equally important.

A Hymn to the Word:
A Hymn to Jesus Christ

The literary context reinforces the conclusion that the preceding hymn is no literary ornament, regardless of whether it is the creation of the author or something incorporated from the traditions of the community. Instead, the hymn is the first crucial ingredient in establishing the emerging identity of Jesus. In the final analysis, it is impossible to say whether the author of the Fourth Gospel was also the poet who crafted language into this song for the people to sing. The artistry of the complex narrative that constitutes this Gospel makes that creative contribution seem quite possible. But the writer also might be like African American preachers who are so steeped in the hymnody of their community that they are able to weave hymns into their sermons to make present again the powerful truths of their faith. Suffice it to say that this particular hymn reaches back into the people's biblical heritage to evoke the ineffable truth that this "only-begotten" child of God incarnates the very heart of God.

The complex christological witness of the hymn in John 1:1–18 is accomplished both by the poetry itself and by the commentary interwoven with it. As rereaders who already know what will follow (a circumstance that the author appears to take for granted in 11:2, for example, where reference is made to Mary's anointing of Jesus recounted a chapter later), we make the connection between the λόγος and Jesus from the outset of the poem, even though he is not mentioned until the end. The result is that God's interaction with the creation is telescoped together, such that the drama of the creation and the arrival of Jesus Christ are seen in a single blink of an eye. The saving work of Christ is thus part of a movement from "the beginning" that flows into a cosmological tale of divine passion and creativity.[4] Regardless of the immediate needs of the Johannine community and the sometimes introverted posture that their experience of crisis (whatever its external causes) produced, this programmatic hymn reflects the pluralistic culture within which that community lived and reminds readers of the universal implications of the Gospel to which it bears witness.[5]

Strophes 1 and 2 (1:1–5):
The Word "In the Beginning"

Rather than setting forth only the "preexistence of the Christ," the first strophe of the poem sets the stage for a story of the continued engagement of the divine Creator with the creation. It accomplishes this in terms reminiscent of what is said about personified Wisdom in the traditions examined in the previous chapter of this study,[6] but with significant twists. We see the λόγος in intimate proximity to God, as is Wisdom in Proverbs 8:22–31; Sirach 1:1, 4; and Wisdom of Solomon 9:4, 9. God cannot be conceived apart from the λόγος.[7] One is transported back in time even before the primordial chaos awaited the shaping of divine speech (Genesis 1), a time when only the λόγος was abiding with—and yet distinct from—God and gave definition to the Creator.[8] Human speech demonstrates its own inadequacy to speak of such matters by the juxtaposition of the images of accompaniment and companionship that distinguish between the λόγος and God (πρὸς τὸν Θεόν) and the affirmation of identity (καὶ θεὸς ἦν ὁ λόγος) that goes beyond any claim made about Wisdom (though Prov. 3:19 and Wisd. Sol. 7:21 come close).[9]

The second strophe (vv. 3–5) completes the picture of the λόγος "in the beginning" of time by portraying the λόγος as God's companion and coworker in creation. With the λόγος comes the illumination that breaks into the undifferentiated pre-creative night, staking a claim to possibility and hope. This portrayal echoes Wisdom's role in creation, and in particular her connection to the gifts of life and light (Prov. 8:22, 27, 35: Sir. 1:4; 4:12; 24:1–22; Wisd. Sol. 7:21, 29–30; 9:1–2), and her role in the contrast between light and darkness (Prov. 1:20–33; 8:32–36; Sir. 24:1–22; Wisd. Sol. 7:29–30). Another link is suggested in verse 4, where the λόγος is identified as the source of life for humankind. Torah is also understood to impart life, and it too is identified as a form of Wisdom's presence (see Sir. 24, for example).

With the second strophe the problem of pronouns is introduced in the English translation of this poem.[10] Should the grammatically masculine pronouns referring to the grammatically masculine word λόγος be translated as "it" or "its," as would normally be the case ("it is misspelled")? Or should those pronouns already be rendered as "he," "him," and "his," as translators have usually done, already drawing the connection to the as yet unmentioned man Jesus? In English—and in other languages that have no grammatical gender or in which the word for "word" has a grammatical gender different from the biological gender of the man Jesus—the poetic tension is usually collapsed into literalism and linear or sequential reasoning. The primordial echoes of the "cosmological tale" are swallowed up by the particular historical moment encompassed by the life of Jesus of Nazareth.

The Witness of John (1:6–9)

The prosaic introduction of "John" (who in 1:31–34 is said to baptize, but who is not given the title of "Baptist" or "Baptizer" as in the Synoptic tradition) seems at first glance to reinforce the conclusion that Jesus is fully in view by this point in the hymn. A closer look, however, calls that conclusion into question. If one holds in abeyance the picture of John as "forerunner" of or "preparer of the way" for Jesus until that role is introduced by the quotation in 1:23 of Isaiah 40:3,[11] one meets John first as one who testifies or bears witness to the light that is already present (vv. 6–8), as well as to the "true light" that was coming into the world (v. 9). In other words, one could interpret John as a messenger of or witness to Wisdom/ ὁ λόγος whose identity was stamped on the creation itself, a role he will continue relative to Jesus as ὁ λόγος (1:26–36). If this suggestion is accepted, then verse 9 stands as the first reference specifically to Jesus, and not to the large chapters of the cosmological tale of Wisdom's presence that preceded him. In other words, verse 9 pulls the reader forward to the final strophe (vv. 14, 16) and its accompanying prose commentary (vv. 15, 17–18).

Strophe 3 (1:10–12b): The Mixed
Reception of the Word in the World

The third strophe clearly echoes Wisdom's redemptive role on behalf of God in the midst of the creation. These verses, however, can be understood in two ways. Either they summarize the narrative of Jesus' fate that will follow in the Gospel, or else they recapitulate the age-old story of the relentless yearning of Wisdom/ ὁ λόγος to be "known" and to find a home among humankind (see, for example, Prov. 1:20–33; 8:1–9:12; Wisd. Sol. 7:24–8:8; Sir. 15:7; chap. 24; Bar. 3:12–23). The need to make a decision about how to render the third person masculine pronouns in English has reinforced the former conclusion, as they point to a male and effectively eclipse the latter reference. In fact, though, the latter seems primary here, given the presence of the verb ἔγνω and the absence of any foreshadowing of the dramatic rejection of Jesus even to the point of his execution.

Those Who Become
God's Children (1:12b–13)

Those who did accept "αὐτόν," and who are given the "authority" (ἐξουσία) to become children of God (see Wisd. Sol. 7:27), are further identified in the prose elaboration that follows the third strophe. Here again pronouns cause a problem for the interpretation. At issue is the referent of αὐτοῦ in verse 12c. The usual assumption is that it refers to the name the λόγος will bear—that is, Jesus. Indeed, in the remainder of the Gospel, references to things occurring or being done "in the name" of Jesus abound (2:23; 3:18; 14:13, 14, 26; 15:16, 21; 16:23, 24, 26; 20:31). Two of these even refer to "believing" in his name (2:23; 3:18). On the other hand, the noun immediately preceding that pronoun in 1:12c is "God." Elsewhere in the Gospel there are no references specifically to the name of God (that is, the noun θεός), but rather the name is linked to God as "my father" (5:43; 10:25) or, in prayer, is specified by the second-person singular pronoun (τὸ ὄνομά σου; 12:28; 17:6; 26). The internal logic of the verse could bear either meaning, namely, that one's being "begotten" by God could be a consequence of one's belief in the "name" of God[12] or of this one in whom God is present. This tension of a double referent once again seems appropriate to this Gospel that affirms both a distinction and no real difference between the Christ and God.

Strophe 4 (1:14, 16, [15]):
The λόγος Becomes Flesh

The final strophe of the poem goes beyond anything said of Wisdom.[13] Wisdom concretized and localized the divine power, order, and animating force for the people of Israel and was often talked about as a female figure, but until Wisdom took on concrete expression in Torah (as in Sirach 24 and Bar. 3:9–4:4), exactly how it appeared is not stated. Wisdom simply appeared, carried out the quest for acceptance and recognition, and then was gone—perhaps returning to the heavenly places of Wisdom's origin. As Torah, Wisdom was present as the life-giving story of God's presence, advocacy, and covenant with God's people, and the equally life-giving guidance for the people's covenant walk with God. The new "tent" of Wisdom's dwelling (σκηνόω) was to be not the grammar and vocabulary of instruction, but the human life of the λόγος. In that human locus, all who recognize the Word's true identity can recognize a glory that embodies God's glory as clearly as an only child re-presents a parent. Clearly at this point the hymn is linked directly to the account of Jesus' words and deeds that constitutes this Gospel. Willett summarizes by saying that "the metaphysical has given way to the historical."[14] Or, perhaps a better way to put it, in appropriately paradoxical language in keeping with the Fourth Gospel, metaphysical truth is carried in the finitude and the historical particularity of the human life of Jesus of Nazareth.

Qualities elsewhere attributed to Wisdom here are ascribed to the incarnate one—glory (Wisd. Sol. 7:22, 25–26; 8:10; 9:11; Sir. 24:16), truth (Prov. 8:6–7; 14:22–23; Sir. 4:24–25), grace[15] (Prov. 18:22; Sir. 24:16), and being the "only begotten" (μονογενής) of God (Wisd. Sol. 7:22). On the other hand, the temporal side of the paradox is supported by the shift from third-person pronouns in the earlier strophes to first-person plural pronouns to identify the ones among whom the incarnate λόγος dwells. "We" now are the witnesses and partakers (v. 16) of the bounty[16] of this divine presence. The testimony attributed to John in verse 15 also links the earlier mention of his witness to ὁ λόγος to his now specific witness to "this one" (οὗτος). While the third-person singular pronouns in this section still refer to the λόγος, their double reference to it and to the man Jesus makes determining their appropriate translation into English an even more difficult decision.

Both "Father" and "Son" as titles for God and Jesus, respectively, are usually introduced into the discussion of the Fourth Gospel in relation to verse 14. In neither case is the reference unambiguous, however. At issue is a description of the "glory" of the λόγος become flesh. That glory is described by an analogy (ὡς): It is compared to the relation of an only child to a "father."[17] Neither term refers directly to God or to Jesus.

A Concluding Commentary
on the Hymn (1:17–18)

Two verses of prose commentary are appended to the hymn to amplify and clarify the final strophe. The first, verse 17, appears to develop the concluding phrase of verse 16. Thus, the terms "law," "grace," and "truth" should be seen as standing in synthetic parallelism[18] to identify the gifts of the λόγος to humankind, whether through Moses or through Jesus Christ. It would be a misreading to see the law as in some way temporary or inferior, falling into irrelevance when the other gifts arrive. After all, the law is identified with Wisdom in such texts as Sirach 24:8–12 and Baruch 3:6–4:1, and Jews (such as the Johannine community) would certainly have understood the law as mediating life. What is puzzling is the implication that grace and truth came only with Jesus Christ and, consequently, that only Jesus Christ can make God known.[19] Perhaps, though, that is also a misreading. Recall that in the final strophe of the poem the emphasis is on the concrete manifestation of ὁ λόγος/Wisdom in flesh, parallel to the concrete manifestation of Wisdom in Torah. The verse then may not be suggesting that grace and truth are absent from Torah, but rather that they are embodied also through this move of the λόγος into flesh. All three of these dimensions of God's life-giving power—Wisdom as encountered in Torah, grace, and truth—are now embodied in this "fullness" that the community has received.

The second part of the concluding commentary (v. 18) goes back to the reference to the δόξα of the incarnate λόγος in verse 14. What is actually revealed or "interpreted" (ἐξάγω) in the λόγος is God.[20] Just as Wisdom is both the manifestation and the presence[21] of God (or one might say "of YHWH"), so now this μονογενὴς Θεός is for ὁ πατήρ (seen also as a circumlocution for the God whose name is too holy to be spoken). "Only-begotten God" is the best translation for this phrase of which both words are in the nominative case. Manuscript evidence indicates that from very early times copyists wrestled with its meaning and tried to interpret it in keeping with belief in Jesus as the son of his divine father.[22] I must conclude, though, that while the intimacy between God and the λόγος that was celebrated in the first strophe of the hymn (vv. 1–2) is clearly being affirmed to continue in Jesus' relationship with God, paternity appears not to be an issue.

And so ends this hymn to the λόγος/Wisdom made flesh. The hymn is never referred to again in the entire Gospel–at least not explicitly. However, the hymn does serve as a prologue to the Gospel by setting forth the theological framework around which the subsequent narrative is woven. Themes central to the hymn in its portrayal of the λόγος are lifted up and turned a bit in new directions as they now take on the flesh of the Incarnate One whose tale is told in the unfolding story of the Gospel.

THE HYMN IN THE REST OF THE GOSPEL

The Motif of the λόγος

The hymn as a whole is about the λόγος. Although that term is never again used in the Fourth Gospel as a christological title, it appears frequently as a motif or unit of thought. Rather than allow the convention of writing "word" with an uppercase initial letter in the prologue and then a lowercase letter in subsequent occurrences to separate their meanings, a more productive route seems to be to take the author at face value in his choice of language, and even to explore associations with related verbs and nouns pointing toward speech, language, or voice.[23]

Many occurrences of these terms carry simple common meanings, such as a passing remark (2:22; 4:39; 7:36), a proverb (4:37; 15:20), vague rumors (21:23), or a specific passage of scripture (12:38) or scripture in general (10:35; 15:25; 18:9). Minear identifies seven passages of the Gospel where these terms are affiliated with other constructions to form clusters that illuminate the importance of the λόγος in delineating not only dimensions of Christology, but also the author's understanding of the church. Those passages can be identified in summary form as follows:

5:19–29 — Wherever Jesus' word or voice is heard, Jesus himself is heard, and his presence mediates the life-giving power that he shares with God. One is included in or excluded from the church on the basis of one's response to that word.

5:30–47 — The λόγος resides in the community, constituting God's own testimony and thereby becoming "one way of discerning the boundary between the community that is faithful to the Mosaic testimony and its counterfeit."[24]

6:52–71 — Jesus' word or words are inseparable from the bread of heaven that has become flesh in Jesus Christ, capable of mediating both death and life. Bread and word alike are central to the relationship of mutual abiding (the verb μένω comes into play here) that unites God, Christ, and believers.

8:31–47 — Response to the λόγος becomes the factor differentiating two communities of people: those who abide in that word and thus are true disciples, and those who seek to kill Jesus because his λόγος finds no place to abide in them.

12:44–50—There is a correlation of word, life, and light, and a similar correlation among hearing, seeing, obeying, and believing. As commandment and as light, the word is linked to the gift of life.

17:6–19—Jesus' giving of the word corresponds to God's gift of "his own" to Jesus. Their keeping of that word (or commandment) unites them with God, Christ, and one another.

17:20–26—The words of those who have first heard and known Jesus' word continue to mediate life in a "chain of glory" that had its origins before the foundation of the world.[25]

In short, where the word or words that proclaim the Gospel are present, the Word of whom the Gospel tells is present too, and in that Word abides the Divine One who sent the Word. The word of proclamation in the Johannine community is thus traced to the Word whose home is with God from the very beginning, and as such, it continues to convey to humanity "God's name, authority, light, glory, truth, life, and love. . . . [Where] God's logos is, there God is."[26]

The evidence in the remainder of the Gospel thus shows the term λόγος to be fully christological in that it is at heart theological in focus, rather than functioning only as a personal title for Jesus. Like Wisdom, the λόγος expresses God's speech/act when "the Word became flesh," just as it has from "the beginning." The Gospel as a whole thus appears to support the analysis presented above: the prologue does not have in view the prehistory of Jesus of Nazareth, but rather the saga of God's yearning for a home among humankind, a yearning conveyed by divine Wisdom in all her guises, including the λόγος become flesh.

Divine Presence and Divine Gifts

The first two strophes of the hymn set forth the intimacy between the λόγος and God and the role of the λόγος in the creation—in particular in the origins of life and light. While nothing is said elsewhere in the Gospel about Jesus as active in the creation of the world, the other motifs of these verses appear frequently. For instance, Jesus' teachings and deeds can be trusted because of the intimacy with God he has enjoyed as the λόγος.[27] Thus, his words and deeds convey what he has seen and learned by having been present with God (3:11–15; 5:19–46; 6:46). If one has known or seen Jesus, one has known God (14:7–14). Jesus shares God's fate, in that those who reject God will reject Jesus as well, and rejecting Jesus amounts to rejecting God (15:18–25). Where Jesus is present, light breaks into and conquers the surrounding darkness (8:12–20; 9:5; 11:9–10; 12:35–36,[28] 46).

The power to mediate life moves into the salvific work of the λόγος carried out by Jesus. He is said to restore physical life to the son of the royal official (4:46–53) and to his friend Lazarus (chap. 11). His authority over life becomes part of the warrant for his action in healing the man by the Sheep Gate Pool (5:21–29, 39–47). Most important of all, he mediates "abundant" or "eternal" life—that life that finally conquers death once and for all (8:51; 10:10, 28; 14:1–4). "Believing" in him, or accepting him as the "bread of life" (6:35–40, 47–51) conveys that life to the community of his disciples, a community that stands as a witness to the power of life in a world more at home with death.

Acceptance and Rejection:
Community Boundaries

The entire Gospel narrative is the story of the interplay of the acceptance and rejection of Jesus. Those who follow him and "remain" with him (and he with them) constitute the insiders of the Johannine community, those born ἄνωθεν as children of God (1:12; 3:1–10). Others reject him (and ultimately his followers as well, as in 15:18–24 and 16:1–4) and bear labels that in this Gospel identify outsiders (principally "the world" and "the Jews"). This dynamic is played out in virtually every segment of this Gospel, but it can be seen with particular clarity in 3:17–21, 31–36; 5:1–18, 39–47; 6:25–66; 7:1–13; 8:31–39; 9:1–41; 10:19, 24, 31; 11:45–53; 12:42–43; and, of course, the passion narrative (chaps. 18–19). Something that is striking about many of these passages is that, despite the generally polemical tone against those who reject Jesus, the double valent—those who accept and those who reject—is sustained. Even the category of οἱ Ἰουδαῖοι includes both groups (see, for example, 10:24, 31; 11:45–53; 12:42–43; and the role of Joseph of Arimathea and Nicodemus in 19:38–41). Thus, Jesus as the incarnate λόγος, like Wisdom, serves as the point of discrimination between insiders and outsiders. In that way, he establishes the boundaries of the community to which this Gospel is addressed. The Gospel, however, expresses no joy over the fact that that line of the third strophe of the introductory hymn is borne out by the rest of the narrative.

Glory and Incarnation

In the Fourth Gospel, the drama of Jesus' double identity as the λόγος and as a human being bearing physical and temporal finitude unfolds with the movement of the narrative. Jesus remains (μένω) with the various groups and individuals he encounters. He demonstrates power to communicate healing and even life itself, but he cannot change hearts that have hardened against him. In the Fourth Gospel, the passion narrative is told in a way that shows Jesus almost presiding over its course, without the picture painted by the Synoptic accounts—especially by Mark's—of the prayerful struggle in Gethsemane or the sense that the process leading to his death is out of his control. Nevertheless, in the Fourth Gospel too Jesus dies, and it is crucial that the reader accept his death as real and not as the shedding of a human disguise by a Gnostic redeemer. The death is real or else the resurrection is not real, and the Fourth Gospel is clear that the one who returns "above" whence he came is also the one resurrected from the dead. In that sense, as Catherine Cory has demonstrated relative to 7:1–8:59, the entire Gospel both tells the story of Wisdom/ὁ λόγος become flesh and is itself a "wisdom tale" that affirms the sovereignty of God against the forces of evil and thus testifies that the protagonist's claims are true and valid.[29]

The affirmation of the final strophe of the poem that "we have seen his glory" bears out the paradox of the double identity that begins the strophe, for the "glory" that is referred to throughout the Gospel belongs in fact to God, and relates principally to Jesus' crucifixion and to events that precipitate it (7:18, 39; 8:50, 54; 11:4; 12:23, 27–29; 13:31–32; 14:13). Far from glory in the fleshly terms of Jesus' life on earth, it reflects the categories of his origin "from above" in the very heart of God and his return by being "lifted up" (3:14) on the cross.

Oddly enough, the "grace" (χάρις) with which he is filled and which "we" now have received (1:14, 16) is never mentioned again in the Fourth Gospel. Perhaps the explanation is that in its place are to be found the two word families related to the love that is embodied in friendship (ἀγαπάω and φιλέω), as is discussed in chapter 5 of this study. In that case, "grace" is no abstraction, but rather it too becomes enfleshed in the exigencies of human relationships. The grace in which we share, then, is Jesus' initiative in calling his followers "friends" and "appointing" them to "appoint" their lives (the verb in both cases is τίθημι) on behalf of one another (15:13, 16).

An additional point from the concluding section of the hymn that needs to be traced in the rest of the Gospel is the reference to Moses and the law in the prose commentary in 1:17. Although occasionally Jesus engages in debate about implications of the law (for example 8:17; 10:34; 12:34; [8:5]), and although he is said to give his followers "a new commandment" or "commandments" that they must obey (13:34; 14:15, 21; 15:10, 12), the Fourth Gospel's view of the law and of Moses is generally positive.[30] Even more than that, one's stance toward Moses is equated with one's acceptance or rejection of Jesus and his teachings (5:45–46; 6:32; 7:19–24). Clearly a polemic is involved in the context of the Johannine community with its majority of Jewish members. The author equates the community's stance of believing in Jesus with faithfulness to their foundations in Judaism (an equation which others apparently do not accept, as is suggested in 9:28–29). Rather than a polemic against Moses, which would probably not have been accepted among that audience, the agenda seems clearly to be to claim to be true heirs of Moses. The evidence of the remainder of the Gospel thus corroborates the reading of 1:17 as synthetic parallelism, and not as a contrast to or a replacement of Moses and the law.

Finally, the Father/Son language referring to God and to Jesus that abounds in the Fourth Gospel is usually traced to this hymn, and, as indicated above, that conclusion is then read into the translation of the hymn itself. For the reasons already stated, I am reluctant to lodge responsibility for that theological decision with the hymn. That is, I am convinced that the Johannine confession of Jesus as the divine Son of God-the-Father was part of the theological stance of the community that shaped the language of the Gospel. What is in fact striking is that such language was not made more explicit in this programmatic hymn. Even if the hymn were a text received by the author with its present language intact, the concluding prose commentary of 1:18 offered ample opportunity for such specificity—for example, by introducing the word υἱός (as later copyists tended to do) or by a possessive pronoun with the word "father." Thus, while Elisabeth Schüssler Fiorenza's conclusion appears correct, namely, that Jesus' identity as Sophia incarnate or even as the son of divine Wisdom has been eclipsed in this Gospel by the doubly mas-culine identity of son of the divine Father,[31] the prologue appears to have been an instance of, rather than a warrant for, that interpretation.

WISDOM'S SAVING PRESENCE

In addition to echoes of the λόγος hymn, other attributes of divine Wisdom also find their way into the proclamation of Jesus and the definition of the community through him in the Fourth Gospel. As has been the case in looking at the testimony to Jesus seen through the hymn, in these attributes also the incarnation of the λόγος in the human male Jesus is a key factor in the transposition of the images from those attributed there to Lady Wisdom. Whether the result should be seen as the affirma-tion of feminine qualities as central to the community's understanding of Jesus, or as the symbolic usurpation by a male of Sophia's role in salvation,[32] is open to de-bate. In any event, attributes or activities of Wisdom that have become powerful motifs in the Gospel narrative are encounters with people on the streets and in pub-lic places (as does Wisdom in Prov. 1:20–33); the pattern of descent (to earth from heaven) followed by ascent (return to dwell with God);[33] teaching the way to life; providing nourishment (Sirach 24); and, finally, the various "I AM" sayings.

Encounters in Public Places

Wisdom's zeal to find those who would accept her, learn from her, and find the life that is God's saving intent for them is poignantly portrayed in her combing the street corners and marketplaces to make her case (for example, Prov. 1:20–33; 8:1–36). Jesus is portrayed as less frenzied than is Wisdom in Proverbs 1:20–33, for example. But it is striking that in the account of his public ministry (John 1–11), only Nicodemus's furtive visit (3:1–21) is engineered to take place under cover. Otherwise, beginning with the accounts of the gathering of the disciples in John 1, Jesus meets, heals, and teaches people outdoors or in overtly public gatherings like the wedding in the village of Cana, which apparently included many of the towns-people (2:1–11). Jesus approaches and teaches the Samaritan woman at the local well (4:4–42). He challenges and heals the paralyzed man by the portico of the temple (5:1–18), and the man born blind meets Jesus walking along the road (9:1–39). The royal official meets him in an undesignated place, but apparently while Jesus is still on the road (4:46–54). He feeds the multitude on a mountain-side (6:1–14) and teaches the disciples and others by the sea (6:25–71). The outer court of the temple where the vendors and money changers ply their trade is the site of prophetic words and actions (2:13–22). Even Mary and Martha's dialogues with Jesus following their brother's death take place when they go to meet him on the way to the house, and not inside (11:20–27, 29–37).[34]

In some cases narrative logic dictates an outdoor setting (the crowds at the meal in 6:1–14), and clearly it is not always Jesus who takes the initiative in the en-counters. Two points of contrast, however, make this detail of public settings suf-ficiently striking to suggest that it should be seen as a part of a deliberate agenda of the author. First, there is the contrast between this motif and the Synoptic tra-ditions that set many events during Jesus' "public" ministry (prior to the passion narrative) in houses and other private spaces (Mark 1:29–31; 2:1–12, 15–17; 4:10–12; 5:35–43; Luke 7:36–50; 10:38–42; 11:1–13; 14:1–24, and others). Second, there is the contrast within the Fourth Gospel between these events and the events with the disciples immediately before Jesus' arrest and the administrative hearings by which he is condemned. In these episodes we find Jesus and the disciples inside — in Mary, Martha, and Lazarus's house in 12:1–8, and in an unidentified place during their final evening together in John 13–17. The disciples by this time are "insiders," both in the physical setting of their meetings with Jesus and, more important, in their being Jesus' own who have received him, for they have come and seen, and Jesus has stayed with them.

From all appearances in this Gospel, the Johannine community itself was focused inward on matters of self-understanding, boundary definition, and even survival, and not actively recruiting other members. The portrait of Jesus constantly, in public places, despite the opposition he is said to have catalyzed, is thus even more striking. Clearly such a vocation belonged to his identity as they confessed him, and not to a projection of an agenda of their own mission. He was, they said, out there like Wisdom herself, making himself known to "his own" in the hope that they would recognize him and follow his way. Again like her, he found that hope more often frustrated than realized.

"Sent from Above"

Jesus meets us in the Fourth Gospel as one who "remains" with us for a time, but whose true home is elsewhere — "above" or "with God" (3:11–21; 7:32–36; 8:21–30; 13:1; 14:1–17, 28–31; 16:7). This home reflects Jesus' origin as much as his destiny, and this combination — where he is going and where he comes from — defines his identity. The title associated in the Fourth Gospel with the descent-then-ascent pattern that links Jesus' origin and destiny is the υἱὸς τοῦ ἀνθρώπου who descended from heaven and thus knows "heavenly things," and must be "lifted up" (on the cross), which will end his sojourn on earth and return him to God (3:11–21). The biblical model being invoked is the "fiery" bronze serpent that Moses lifted up on a pole (LXX, σημεῖον) as an instrument of redemption for Israelites who looked at it when they were menaced by the plague of "fiery" biting serpents that conveyed God's anger with the people (Num. 21:6–9). Similarly, in the logic of this Gospel, the Human One, whose vocation in Ezekiel is to convey a prophetic message from God to the people and in Daniel is to mediate the judgment by God of humankind, is transformed into one who conveys not judgment, but eternal life to those who accept him. The "lifting up" that clearly looks forward to the cross at the same time provides the key to interpreting the "signs" (σημεῖα) that Jesus performs (2:11, 23; 4:54; 6:2, 14; 7:31; 9:16; 11:47; 12:18, 37; 20:30). They are first and foremost not wonders or "miracles," but rather actions that point toward and narratively lead toward the cross, whose form is also a σημεῖον.

In addition to the explicit link to the figure of the Human One, the pattern of one whose origin is with God and who is sent to convey God's gift and purpose of life parallels the earthly sojourn of divine Wisdom. Like her, Jesus is sent from

God (5:38; 7:18, 28–29; 12:44; 13:20), and he is sent to save "the world," even though only some respond to him (3:16–17; 5:34; 10:9; 12:47).

The magnetic attraction pulling Jesus back to his place of origin leaves his followers on earth facing the risk of losing their connection to the one who has been their connection to "eternal" life. Reassurance thus becomes the refrain of the final discourse of Jesus (John 13–17) in particular. He goes to prepare a place for them with him (14:1–7), and he promises the "other παράκλητος" to accompany them still on earth (14:26; 16:13–14). The Fourth Gospel thereby resolves the dilemma posed by the Wisdom traditions—how to affirm both Wisdom's abiding home (with God) and defining vocation (continuing to mediate God's redemptive presence among humankind).

Teacher of Wisdom's Way

All four Gospels agree in presenting Jesus as the consummate teacher. In the Fourth Gospel he is called "teacher" (or "rabbi") in 1:38; 3:2; 8:4; 13:12–14; 20:16. The verb is associated with his actions in 6:59; 7:14–24; 8:2, 20, 28; 18:20, and his teaching will be complemented by the other παράκλητος according to 14:26 and 16:4–15. The long farewell discourse of John 13–17 resembles a legacy conveyed by a wise teacher to followers in a private teaching before the teacher's death. His almost catechetical conversation with Martha (11:21–27) and his repeated question to Peter in 21:15–19 ("Do you love me?"), which clearly sought understanding and not simple assent, also portray Jesus as a teacher of those who were able to learn from him. The earthly Jesus teaches using proverbs (12:24–25) and figures of speech (10:1–18; 15:1–11) typical of wisdom literature,[35] and even the beatitude attributed to the risen Christ (20:29) fits such a literary classification.

Closely related to the attribution of wisdom speech forms to Jesus is the pattern of riddles and misunderstandings that mark Jesus' encounters with such characters as the woman of Samaria and Nicodemus. The author's point is not to contrast Jesus' cleverness and the others' stupidity, but rather to present a search for understanding through a Socratic pattern of misunderstanding and correction that fits well in the genre of wisdom literature. In a similar way the long discourses after the healings of the people who are blind (John 5 and 7) and paralyzed (John 9 and 10) turn also on double entendres and unwitting truths, as Jesus' identity as judge, giver of life, good shepherd, and vine unfolds.

More than simply a great teacher, Jesus, like Wisdom, conveys by his very life the order and meaning inherent in God's own nature and communicated by the creator into the creation itself, and now into God's redemptive presence as well. Thus, the account of Jesus' life shapes the rhythms of the community's life by schematizing time through the Jewish festivals that are reread to interpret and contextualize events in his own life (Sabbath: 5:9; 9:14; Dedication: 10:22; the Feast of Booths: 7:2; and Passover: 2:13, 23; 6:4; 11:55). This logic of time restores a piece of the meaningful universe that is under threat for John's community if their continued participation in the life of the synagogue is in jeopardy.

Although nothing in this Gospel suggests that the Johannine community was experiencing a sense of separation from God's blessings conveyed in the narrative and instruction found in the Torah, Jesus is portrayed as becoming for them a "way" (14:4–6) and as giving them a new "commandment" (13:34; 14:15–17, 21; 15:10, 12–17), which he also embodies in his own life. Jesus is thus the consummate teacher of wisdom in the sense of the canon by which to order one's life. He echoes and reinforces Moses, through whom Torah was handed down to them. But he then goes a step further by giving them his own life as a new story of God's grace, power, and justice. As the incarnation of the divine λόγος, that life truly discloses the logic of the whole world in the Wisdom of the creator's own heart.

Wisdom's Bounty

The traditions about divine Wisdom are replete with images of Wisdom sharing the divine bounty, preparing food and water for the blessing and well-being of the people (Prov. 9:5; 13:14; 16:22; 18:4; 20:5; Sir. 15:3; 24:19–21, 25–27, 30–33; Wisd. Sol. 7:11, 14). Jesus is portrayed as similarly committed to mediating food, drink, and refreshing water as the gifts of God for the people of God.[36] For example, just as Sophia mixes wine for the people, Jesus provides abundant and excellent wine for a wedding banquet in the first of the "signs" that point the way to the cross (2:1–11), a journey that testifies to the fact that many among his own people are not able to receive the bounty he offers, just as her own disregard and even discard Wisdom. That theme is sustained in the account of the feeding of the multitude in 6:1–14, which is followed by the discourse in which Jesus claims not just to give, but also to become the "bread of life" (6:25–65). Having been a guest at a dinner party at the home of his friends in 12:1–8, he takes over in a dramatic way the role of a gracious host during the final evening he shares with his disciples (13:1–20).

At a well in Samaria, Jesus encounters a woman who on the basis of his insight and commentary comes to recognize him and carry his story to her people (4:4–42). To her he offers the "water of life," which—unlike the food and water Wisdom gives according to Sirach 24:21—will leave her never to thirst again.[37] His gift of water to those who thirst is announced again in 7:37–39, as he becomes himself the source of this symbol of God's blessing and deliverance of the people (Num. 20:2–13; Isa. 12:3; 44:3; 55:1).

ἐγώ εἰμι

With his both giving and becoming the bread of life, Jesus' representation of Wisdom's role of sharing the divine bounty overlaps the final group of Wisdom motifs that will be explored, namely, the cluster of "I AM" sayings. I write the phrase with both words in uppercase letters to indicate that the term refers to a variety of sayings with an expressed pronoun as the subject. Since the pronominal subject is conveyed by the verb form itself, an expressed subject usually indicates contrast ("I say this, but you say that") or emphasis ("*You* may have said that, but it is not true").

The ἐγώ εἰμι sayings in the Fourth Gospel fall into two categories. One group has a variety of complements (bread of life, true vine, good shepherd, and so forth), and the other group has none and is usually rendered in English by something like

"I am he." The uncomplemented form of the saying occurs in John 4:26; 6:20; 8:24, 28, 58; 13:19; and 18:5, 6, 8. In each case, it is used by Jesus to acknowledge an attribute or identity attributed to him by other characters in the narrative. In other words, the meaning fits the emphatic use of the expressed subject pronoun. Within the narrative, we are not told the response of the other characters to this phrase in most cases. Three exceptions, however, suggest that the author is engaging the reader in a game of double entendre in which more is being said than meets the eye. The speech in which the phrase occurs in 8:28 evokes a response of faith in 8:30 (πολλοὶ ἐπίστευσαν εἰς αὐτόν). In 8:58 opponents immediately pick up stones to throw at him. In 18:6 the onlookers fall to the ground. These responses point toward a dramatic claim being conveyed by the phrase—in fact, apparently, a claim of Jesus' divinity. Although in Exodus 3:14 where the divine name is given, the LXX uses ὁ ὤν, meaning something like "the Existent One,"[38] it is clear from the LXX of such texts as Isaiah 43:25; 45:18; 48:12; 51:12; and 52:6 that ἐγώ εἰμι was also a code for the divine name among Greek-speaking Jews. The phrase—particularly when it has no complement—weaves through the Gospel the affirmation made in the λόγος hymn of Jesus' "past eternity and future imperishability,"[39] now present in human flesh.

The statements in which ἐγώ εἰμι is followed by various complements both make claims about the meaning of Jesus and amplify the first group of such sayings by expressing deity through metaphor or similitude.[40] In these statements Jesus is identified as the bread of life (6:35, 48); the light of the world (8:12; 9:5); the gate to the sheepfold (10:7, 9); the good shepherd (10:11); the way, the truth, and the life (14:4–6); and the true vine (15:1). These various terms indicate not changes in Jesus' identity as the Gospel unfolds, but rather an accumulation of meaning that is revealed. All of them except the "good shepherd" are explicitly associated with Wisdom ("bread" in Sir. 24:21; the "vine" in Sir. 24:17, 19;[41] the "way" in Prov. 3:17; 8:32; Sir. 6:26; "light" in Wisd. Sol. 7:26; 18:34; "truth" in Prov. 8:7; Wisd. Sol. 6:22; "life" in Prov. 3:18; 8:38; and even the "gate of the sheep" that parallels Wisdom's door as the way to life in Prov. 8:34–35).[42] The various attributes relate also in a more general way to Sophia as the one who gives the people nourishment and other necessities of life, who protects them from all danger, and who is identified with the sage management of life as both wise counsel and Torah, the quintessential "way" to life (Pss. 119:30; 136:11; Prov. 5:6; 6:23; Tob. 1:3; Wisd. Sol. 5:6; Sir. 24:25).[43] According to the Fourth Gospel, though, Jesus exceeds Wisdom's power to mediate life in its fullness. Wisdom indeed spreads a banquet for her people, but Jesus becomes their food for life. He is at the same time their companion, both during his life and when he comes as the "other παράκλητος"—sharer of the way, the truth, bread, and the life that he himself has become.

CONCLUSION

The foregoing study shows that the hymn that begins the Fourth Gospel echoes throughout the Gospel. The echoes of that hymn are complemented by a variety of additional motifs that show that the Wisdom traditions found in the Hebrew

Bible and in the deuterocanonical literature constitute a significant resource for the Christology of the Fourth Gospel. Just as Wisdom had some people who accepted her and her teachings and others who refused to receive her, so also was the case with the λόγος who became flesh according to the Fourth Gospel. Those who accepted the λόγος became the new community of "children" (1:12) or "friends" (15:12–17) of God. In that way, Wisdom (now become flesh) serves as a criterion that defines the center and the boundaries of the community as well.

A question that remains unresolved in this study is how to understand issues of gender raised by this affirmation that Wisdom is called by the masculine term ὁ λόγος and said to be made flesh in a male human being. Should we conclude, with Scott, that Jesus is the incarnation of both female and male principles of the divine, and that in him both dimensions are preserved?[44] Or should we perhaps join Raymond Brown who says that in this Gospel Jesus is portrayed as "the supreme example of divine Wisdom active in history, and indeed divine Wisdom itself"?[45] Or could we accept the eloquence of Elizabeth Johnson when she speaks of the way the Fourth Gospel maintains the tension of the "female symbol" of Wisdom or Sophia known in the human male, Jesus? She makes her case as follows:

> Since Jesus the Christ is depicted as divine Sophia, then it is not unthinkable — it is not even unbiblical — to confess Jesus the Christ as the incarnation of God imaged in female symbol. Whoever espouses a wisdom Christology is asserting that Jesus is the human being Sophia became; that Sophia in all her fullness was in him so that he manifests the depth of divine mystery in creative and graciously saving involvement in the world.[46]

Or, on the opposite side, should we join our voices with others, like Luise Schottroff, Elisabeth Schüssler Fiorenza, and Judith E. McKinley,[47] who conclude that the grammatically masculine λόγος and the male Jesus have so eclipsed "Lady Wisdom" that not only her grammatical presence but even her feminine traits and female roles have been thoroughly co-opted and masculinized? The arguments on both sides are persuasive, and perhaps the best that can be said is that our understanding of both Wisdom and Jesus Christ are transformed — the first by the saga of the incarnation, and the second by the feminine (even female) qualities by which his divine identity is defined.

Although it is clear that a number of the points identified as motifs of Wisdom are far from unique to John among the early proclaimers of Jesus as the Christ, the picture has become exceptionally clear in the Fourth Gospel. While it is risky to claim to know authorial intent when the author has given us only the results and not the rationale for his or her work, it is possible to extrapolate from what we can know about the circumstances of a community's life to the questions, concerns, needs, and hopes that shape their religious life. In the case of John's community, threat of separation from their religious home in the synagogue would have been an experience of dislocation and disorientation. The very structure of their world would have seemed to have come unglued. If such a community were to recognize a word of good news in the story of Jesus and of the community called into being around him, that word would have to call into being a world that holds together even in the face of evidence and a logic of disorder. Jesus as Wisdom/ὁ λόγος become flesh would need to address basic human needs of safety in the face of danger, bread to satisfy deep hunger, water in a thirsty land, underlying wisdom in the face of chaos, and life itself—abundant life—that overcomes death. When the synagogue no longer functions as a reliable home for the Johannine community, the company of those whom Jesus called "friends" becomes that home. In the new commandment that they befriend one another as he has befriended them is born both a new community and a new connection to God that is life itself. There, and in that place prepared for them when Jesus returns whence he came (14:1–7), can be found the many dwelling places of God that are reliable homes for all eternity.

Chapter 5

Appointed to Be Friends

Everyone knows what it means to have a friend and even to be a friend. The term presents a problem less of understanding than of practice. Friends occupy the relational territory somewhere between "family"—those to whom we are related by birth or specific covenants like marriage—and "associates" with whom we have in common only mutual involvement in external tasks or locations (work, commerce, neighborhoods, and so forth). We think of friends as people we "like," people we choose to spend time with, people we care about. If the truth be told, in much of western society of the late twentieth century, friendship seems like a trivial term. "He's just a friend" relegates the person in question to a place removed from the center of one's life. If you are a visitor in a church that calls itself "friendly," someone might actually speak to you at the coffee hour after the service. When the Jesus of the Fourth Gospel is said to have called his disciples "friends," and then to connect that term to a commandment that they be willing to commit their very lives on one another's behalf, just as he has done on their behalf (15:12–17), the text brings us up short. This is far removed from the declaration of Charlie Brown, that icon of popular culture and frequent protagonist of the "Peanuts" comic strip: "A friend is someone who likes you!"

The sayings on friendship in John 15 and the vocabulary of friendship—the noun φίλος and the related verb φιλέω—throughout the Gospel (and especially in the farewell discourse of John 13–17) establish the relevance of the theme to the Fourth Gospel. This study begins, therefore, with an examination of that vocabulary and a close reading of that key text.[1] Further analysis of the role of friendship as a central category of the author's theological thought and as a factor in the literary structure of the Fourth Gospel can only proceed, however, after a brief overview of perspectives on friendship in Hellenistic philosophy and in the biblical traditions that appear to have informed the evangelist's work. Such an overview will contextualize the meaning of friendship in the author's world (rather than ours) and thus enable us to identify ways the theme comes to expression in the Fourth Gospel that go beyond those suggested by its common-sense meaning in the modern world.

LINGUISTIC EVIDENCE: φιλέω, φίλος

The explicit vocabulary of friendship—the noun φίλος and the verb φιλέω—is found throughout the Fourth Gospel. If one includes in the tally of evidence the virtually synonymous verb ἀγαπάω, the language of friendship sounds a persistent beat from the beginning to the end of the narrative. The frequent occurrence of that vocabulary provides one important baseline from which to explore more broadly the motifs and the phenomenon of friendship in the theology of the Fourth Gospel.

The noun designates John the Baptist's relationship to Jesus as "friend" of the bridegroom, or what today would be called the "best man" (3:29), an important but still secondary position in the festivities.[2] The noun also occurs in a threatened accusation against Pilate in 19:12 ("If you release this man, you are not Caesar's friend . . ."). This reference is clearly to the political dimension of friendship—to designate a patron-client relationship in general, and in particular one's loyalty to the emperor. The point is that Pilate ought to take a stand against this person identified as hostile to the emperor, and thus show himself to be like Sejanus, Pilate's overseer, whom Tacitus called a "friend of Caesar" (*Annals* 6.8). The same Sejanus eventually lost favor, however, and the implication is that if Pilate did not oppose someone whose power competed with Caesar's, he too would lose his treasured status.[3] The noun "friend" also refers to Jesus' followers. In John 11, Lazarus of Bethany is called Jesus' friend, and the word is applied to those whom Jesus addresses in the context of the love commandment in 15:12–17.

The verb φιλέω is even more common. Whatever may have been the distinctions in the degree of self-interest conveyed by φιλέω and ἀγαπάω for some writers, for the author of the Fourth Gospel the two terms appear to be synonyms.[4] Both are used to name God's love for Jesus or the Father's for the Son (3:35; 5:20; 10:17; 15:9; 17:23, 24, 26), Jesus' love for members of the family from Bethany (11:3, 5), and God's love for the disciples (16:27; 17:23), and to refer to the disciple whom Jesus "loved" (13:23; 19:26; 20:1; 21:7, 20). Both are found in the triple question and response in the dialogue between Peter and the risen Christ in 21:15, 16, 17. In 15:12–17, the passage where the disciples are called Jesus' "friends" (φίλοι), the verb ἀγαπάω identifies the love for one another that Jesus commands (15:12, 17; see also 13:34). The same verb is used elsewhere to name both Jesus' love for those whom he will call "friends" (13:1; 15:9), and their love for him (14:15, 21, 23, 24, 28).

KEY TEXT: JOHN 15:1–17

The centrality of friendship language in John 15:12–17 allows this passage to function as a lens through which to view the theme in the Fourth Gospel as a whole. This passage is found near the middle of the collection of sayings presented as a farewell discourse (John 13–17) set by John at the final meal shared by Jesus and the disciples. The setting just before Jesus' death and the central role played by various exhortations to care for one another establishes a formal similarity between this and other farewell discourses or speeches anticipating the death of a leader such as Moses (Deut. 30:16), Abraham (*Jub.* 20:2; 21:5; 36:3–4), Joseph (*Test. Jos.* 17:3), and Zebulon (*Test. Zeb.* 8:5–6).[5]

The theme of love operates on at least three levels in that discourse. The first is the redemptive power of Jesus' love for his own that unites them to him and to God for all eternity. The theme of love in John 15 thus echoes the introduction to the discourse in 13:1: " . . . having loved his own who were in the world, he loved them to the end." Second, Jesus' love for the disciples is a pastoral message of comfort for his followers (and for the church in later generations) accompanying the triumphal announcement of Jesus' "glorification" (13:31–32) that is echoed throughout the discourse.[6] Finally, love as a commandment from Jesus amplifies the "example" (13:15) of servant love seen in the foot washing (13:3–17) that Jesus sets as a model for relationships within the community. The foot washing and the new commandment are related as two facets of the same instruction by which their knowledge of and relationship to God are demonstrated to the world.[7]

The portion of the discourse within which the passage on loving one another is found (14:25–15:25) is in the form of a chiasmus, with the central section (15:1–17) framed by two sections that focus on the pastoral implications of Jesus' leave-taking. The first of the framing passages introduces the figure of the παράκλητος (14:25–31), and the second contains warnings about the hostility of the world toward Jesus' followers (15:18–25). The central section begins with the figure of the vine and branches (vv. 1–6). That figure is elaborated and applied to the disciples in verses 7–11, and then expanded to a commandment with a christological base in verses 12–17. Raymond Brown suggests that the application of the figure and its expansion can be seen as a chiasmus, as follows:

vv. 7–10		**vv. 12–17**	
If my words remain in you	(7)	This I command you	(17)
Ask . . . it will be done	(7)	God will give what you ask	(16)
Bear fruit	(8)	Bear fruit	(16)
Becoming my disciples	(9)	I chose you	(16)
God has loved me	(9)	I revealed all I heard from God	(15)
I have loved you	(9)	I have called you my beloved	(15)
You will remain in my love if you keep my commandments	(10)	You are the ones I love when you do what I command	(14)
		My commandment: love one another	(12)

I have said this to you so that
my joy may be yours . . . [8]   (11)

Not only are the details of the parallelism clear, but this structure that recognizes verse 11 as the hinge of the passage highlights the christological center of this pastoral and ethical section of the Gospel. The commandment that both constitutes the church and defines the ethics of the community flows from the fulfillment (indicated by the verb πληρόω) of Jesus' joy and purpose.

Several common motifs link verses 12–17 to both of the previous sections of John 15. First, the preeminence of God (ὁ πατήρ) is affirmed in each (vv. 1, 9, 15,

16). It is God on whom the life of the vine depends; it is God who initiates the love *for* Jesus (objective genitive) that he passes on to the others (subjective genitive); and it is God who is the source of all that Jesus makes known to them. Second, the theme of "abiding" (μένω) is a relationship essential to life: The disciples must abide or remain in Jesus as the branches abide in the vine (vv. 4, 5, 6, 7). More-over, the disciples must abide in Jesus' love, just as he abides in God's love (vv. 9, 10), in order that their "fruit" also should abide (v. 16). The third motif tying to-gether the three sections of 15:1–17 is the "word" or "commandment" that both gives life and carries its own commission (vv. 3, 7, 10, 12, 14, 17). Finally, the love in which they are to abide is spelled out as also the content of Jesus' com-mandment to them. They are to love one another as he loved them. For Jesus this means a total identification with their cause, even to the radical degree of "ap-pointing" (τίθημι) his life on their behalf. By participating in this love for one an-other, they show themselves to be his friends (vv. 12–17).[9]

The love commandment itself depends on the priority of God's love and on the empowering of remaining or abiding in Jesus (and of him in God). It is thus clear that this friendship is contingent, not on the disciples' obedience, but on God's prior love. Thus, "you are my friends" in verse 14 is parallel to "You will remain in my love" in verse 10. Both statements make profound christological claims. At issue is not the ontological nature of Christ (which Martin Dibelius rightly finds lacking here).[10] Instead the christological point is made by analogy with human experience and, simultaneously, linked with the ethical situation in the commu-nity. The love commandment establishes incontrovertibly that for the author of the Fourth Gospel Christology and ethics (and in particular the life of the community of Jesus' followers) are inseparable.[11] Jesus himself embodies friendship, partic-ularly in the approaching passion or "hour" that overshadows the entire farewell discourse. This self-engagement incarnates the life-giving love of God affirmed in John 3:16, and it forms the basis for the claim in 1 John 3:16: "By this we know love, that he appointed his life for us; and we ought to appoint our lives for one another" (author's translation). More than simply a moral paradigm, Jesus is the lover/friend whose love effects life in the beloved by granting them an intimacy with God that itself can be called friendship with God. The effect of Jesus' love is thus parallel to the work of Wisdom who "in every generation . . . passes into holy souls and makes them friends (φίλοι) of God" (Wisd. Sol. 7:27).

In the Fourth Gospel the title "friends" refers to all believers, and not to an elite within the wider Christian community. It would be an error to find here the sug-gestion that such φίλοι contrast with other δοῦλοι on the basis of the superior un-derstanding or knowledge of the former. The title "friends" was indeed used as an in-group designation among the Gnostics to refer to those united to the redeemer, to whom the redeemer reveals everything, and who (like the Christians of John's community) were under the obligation to love one another.[12] The factor that dis-tinguishes the understanding of friendship in John from that in Mandaean thought is that in John that designation is based on Jesus' action (15:13) and not on reve-lation which the adherents themselves have acquired directly.[13] That christologi-cal foundation supports a striking equality of status among members of the community that is corroborated by the absence of even such titles of authority as "apostle" in this Gospel. As Ernst Käsemann concludes, "If all are disciples, brothers, and friends of Jesus, then differentiations among them can no longer be decisive."[14]

While it is clear that the title "friends" does not carry an exclusive sense in the Fourth Gospel, debate continues among scholars about how to understand the commandment to "love one another." Should it be read in a restrictive way, detailing the responsibility of Christians only to those within their community? Or is it a reformulation that does not back away from the radical love of "neighbors" (οἱ πλησίοι) and even "enemies" (οἱ ἔχθροι) commanded in the Synoptic Gospels (Matt. 22:39//Mark 12:31// Luke 10:27; Matt. 4:44//Luke 6:27)?

Most commentators answer the last question in the affirmative: The Fourth Gospel has moved from inclusiveness of responsibility toward "conventicle ethics" that focus inward on the community, even in opposition to outsiders who represent a threat to the community's identity and integrity.[15] That conclusion demonstrates a common-sense logic. Both "one another" as the object of love and "friends" as the term for those for whom one is to commit one's life point in that direction. In popular usage and in much philosophical reflection alike, "friends" suggests partiality. If some are friends, others are not. Indeed, as the discussion below demonstrates, that connotation was current in both the biblical and the secular writings on friendship against which the Fourth Gospel must be read.

There is, however, also another current in that background, which is reflected in narratives about friendship rather than arguments about its meaning or rules for its application. That current develops befriending as a verbal, active notion. The focus is on what a friend does, rather than who qualifies as a legitimate object of one's friendship. At issue is not whom to have as a friend, but how to be a friend. The author approaches friendship from that perspective in John 15:12–17. Friendship is limited not by the definition of its object, but by the difficult and demanding life it entails. Fernando Segovia captures this point well when he observes the twofold dimension of the rhetorical situation in 15:1–17. The disciples are first seen in a positive light, privileged as Jesus' friends. That designation, however, is not a privilege that inheres in some aspect of their identity as objects of Jesus' affection. In the blink of an eye they are recognized to be in need of urgent exhortation about the danger of not bearing fruit. Their discipleship needs constant exercise and validation, both relative to their connectedness to Jesus and in their behavior as friends. Indeed, the author appears to consider the internal danger of their lack of "fruitfulness" to be as great or greater than any external threat to the community.[16]

Seen from this perspective, the Fourth Gospel does not represent a less radical formulation of the love commandment than that found in the Synoptic Gospels. The Synoptic traditions appear still to be in dialogue with the view that links friendship to the patron-client system. Loving one's neighbor or even enemy both expands the boundaries of those eligible to be considered as friends and calls into question the motive of self-interest that undergirds friendship under that system. By making Jesus' own behavior the norm of love commanded to the disciples, however, the Fourth Gospel expands the action of friendship to a christological category.[17] As God's love encompassed "the world" (3:16), and it was for the world that Jesus Christ was sent or appointed, so the love that mirrors the love of Christ likewise knows no limits.

FRIENDSHIP INTERPRETED: EVIDENCE FROM CULTURE

While the presence of the vocabulary of friendship and its christological foundation in John 15:12–17 establish the importance of that theme in the Fourth Gospel, further exploration is needed to suggest the nuances of its meaning, and to alert readers to its development elsewhere in the Gospel. Various biblical (and deuterocanonical) texts dealing with friendship and the writings of various Hellenistic philosophers constitute the territory to be examined. Since none of these sources is actually cited in the Fourth Gospel, they should be recognized as constituting a general background or atmosphere on which the author appears to have drawn, rather than as the basis for specific textual interpretation. Because at least the core of the community to which the Fourth Gospel was directed was Jewish, we can be reasonably certain that the author of the Gospel and the members of his community would have been familiar with the biblical materials related to friendship. We can surmise that it is *likely* that members of the community would also have been familiar with the discussions of friendship among popular philosophers that have found their way into the philosophical writings of the Hellenistic world, simply because such discussions would have taken place on the porches and in the ateliers of such cities as that where the community was located. That familiarity, however, cannot be established with certainty. The biblical material thus must receive the principal focus, even though the theme is more broadly represented in the philosophical writings of the period.

Hellenistic Philosophy[18]

The most familiar discussions of friendship among the philosophers address questions of the value of friendship and the qualities possessed by a person considered as a friend. According to many Hellenistic philosophers, friendship is among the richest of human relationships. They call friendship a virtue (Aristotle, *Nicomachean Ethics* VIII.i.1), and they portray in vivid imagery the value of particular friends. Friendship or filial love was said to consist of mutual respect, trust, care, and goodwill between persons. (Actually one could aptly say between "men," since accounts of women's friendships did not find their way into the common coinage of religious or philosophical literature.) It both improves the quality of life and is a value in and of itself. Thus, Seneca affirms that a wise person can do without friends but does not desire to do so. Rather, such a person desires friends for the purpose of practicing friendship (*Of a Happy Life* xviii).

Most common among the discussions of the philosophers are reflections on various types of friendship as determined by the motives undergirding it—profit, pleasure, or commitment to the well-being of the other, for example. The political sort of friendship that expresses the patron-client relationships that were a basis of life under Roman imperial domination receives the lion's share of attention, even

though it is scorned by the philosophers who discuss it. Questions of the useful-
ness of friends in themselves or to broker one's advancement with more powerful
patrons figure prominently in these discussions (see, for example, Cicero, *De Amicitia* 26–32; *De Natura Deorum* 1.22). The term "friends" also is used to designate members of a religious circle, the followers of a particular philosopher, or
other members of an in-group.[19] More familiar to modern readers are discussions
of friendship as a personal or affective relationship, possible with only a few people at a time, with the ideal being a pair of friends committed to each other in every
possible circumstance of life (Plutarch, *Moralia,* "On Having Many Friends"). Although philosophers most often speak of men who live as friends, husbands and
wives also function as examples of friends, as do pairs of lovers involved in trav-
els and adventures in pursuit of their love.[20]

The Fourth Gospel spends no time cataloguing types of friendship or identifying worthy and unworthy friends, but rather deals with the actions of friends (loving one another, committing their life to one another, and so forth). Given that
focus of the author's attention, it is important to concentrate in this review on what
the philosophers identify as the principal behaviors associated with friendship in
the world from which this Gospel emerged.

For the Hellenistic philosophers the value of friendship undergirds all of human life (Cicero, *De Amicitia* 22), and it comes powerfully into play in situations
of extreme danger or need. For example, Cicero echoes Plato (in the *Lysis*) and
Aristotle (in the *Nicomachean Ethics* VIII.ix.2) in saying that friends have both
goods and experiences — all of life — in common. Friends, says Cicero, share public and private cares, live under the same roof, serve in the same military cam-
paigns. To look on a friend is to look on the image of oneself (Cicero, *De Amicitia*
23). Friendship begins among the strongest and least needy people and is expressed by the mutuality of giving and receiving between friends. Aristotle too emphasizes the mutuality of friendship, but as related to justice and hence central both
to the life of the individual and to the quality of the community (*Eudemian Ethics*
VII.i.3–5; *Nicomachean Ethics* VIII.i.4). He also maintains that friendship levels
the distinctions between unequal partners, even that which is usually drawn between slave and free. Aristotle maintains that, while one cannot have friendship
with a slave as slave, one can as a human being (*Nicomachean Ethics* VIII.xi.7).
Distinctions thus can remain in the social arena, but insofar as the relationship between the parties is one of friendship, the distinctions otherwise in effect are not
relevant. Aristotle also talks of the dilemma that occurs around one friend, who is
also a "good man," and who has not entered into friendship only out of self-
interest. Such a friend, he says, would come readily to the aid of another in a time
of need. That aid would bring comfort to the friend being helped, but it would bring
him additional pain also, out of empathy for the friend who must witness a friend's
pain. Nevertheless a friend goes readily to the aid of another friend who is in need
(see the discussion in Aristotle, *Eudemian Ethics* VII.xi, for example).

Philosophers seem to agree that readiness to accept responsibility for the wel-
fare of a friend or a friend's family members, or even to take risks or to suffer on
behalf of a friend, is basic to that relationship. When philosophers attempt to talk

about these dimensions of friendship—even when they begin with definitions and criteria for recognizing either friends or the behavior of friends—they are quickly reduced to telling stories in which friendship is evidenced. For example, in Lucian's *Toxaris,* several anecdotes illustrate the vocation of one friend to aid another who is in danger or difficulty, even to the point of risking one's own safety.[21] Family obligations, and particularly the care of dependent family members, are assumed by a friend (*Toxaris* 22, 24–26). In mourning or suffering, friends do not shrink from sharing each other's lot, from caring for one another in times of illness, or even from—in two vivid examples—giving one's own eyes to ransom a friend taken prisoner of war (*Toxaris* 40) or putting oneself in the place of a friend about to be eaten by a lion (*Toxaris* 44). Many philosophers identify the supreme duty of a friend as readiness to commit one's life on behalf of a friend, even to the point of death (Aristotle, *Nicomachean Ethics* IX.8; the letter of Epicurus to Diogenes Laertius 121; Epictetus, *Enchiridion* 32.3; Philostratus, *Apollonius of Tyana* vii.14; Lucian, *Toxaris* 7). In that vein, Seneca observes that to have a friend is to have someone for whom one may die or at least pledge one's life ("On Philosophy and Friendship," *Ad Lucilium Epistulae Morales*). Also using language of friendship, Plato claims, "Only those who love wish to die for others" (*Symposium* 179b).

By connecting friendship with readiness to risk one's life for a friend, and at the same time with common elements of daily life (Aristotle, *Nicomachean Ethics* VIII.iii.8), these writings from Greek and Hellenistic philosophers find many echoes in the Fourth Gospel's story of Jesus and his "friends." The forms that these discussions of friendship take among the philosophers—a blend of principles and arguments with narratives illustrating the conduct of friends—suggest another point of comparison with the Fourth Gospel. They push us to look into the stories that are told about Jesus, as well as the specific "love commandment" and other declarative statements about friendship, to discern the role of friendship in the author's literary, christological, and ecclesiological project.

Biblical Examples

Linguistic Evidence. In stark contrast to the prominence of friendship as a theme among Hellenistic philosophers, the language of the Hebrew Bible has no specific word for "friend." Biblical writers spoke rather of neighbors and kin. Occasionally in the LXX, φίλος is used to express various kinship relations, but it occurs principally in the originally Greek texts of the LXX. In several other texts Alexandrian translators, thinking in Hellenistic categories, introduced the word φίλος for מרע—"friend," "companion," or a bridegroom's escort—and φιλία to render the abstract noun רע to mean "desire," "aim," or "purpose."[22]

Despite the lack of a rich vocabulary for friendship in biblical Hebrew, the phenomenon of friendship does play a role in the biblical traditions. Both within the Bible (Isa. 41:8; 2 Chron. 20:7; James 2:23) and in extracanonical writings (*Jub.* 19:9; *Apoc. Abr.* 9:6; 10:6; *Test. Abr.* 13:6; Philo, *Sobr.* 56), Abraham is called a "friend of God,"[23] as are also other patriarchs and Moses himself (see, for example, *Jub.* 30:20; Philo, *Mos.* I, 156),[24] and Israelites who uphold Torah (*Avot* VI:1). At several points in the wisdom literature, and in particular in Proverbs and

Sirach, one finds discussions similar to those in the philosophers about what makes a good or a bad friend, the dangers of friendship entered for dubious motives, and similar issues (see, for example, Prov. 17:17; 18:24; 27:6; Eccles. 4:9–12; Sir. 6:5–17; 9:10–16; chaps. 13–17; 22:19–26; 27:16–21; 37:1–6). In the midst of such rules in Sirach, friendship is viewed as a gift from God and a symbol of divine-human communion. Thus, the quality of one's human friendships should express the quality of one's relationship with God, and those who "fear God" can have friendship both with God and with others.[25] The words on friendship in Ecclesiastes 4:9–12 speak cynically of utilitarian friendship as a prescription to ease life's pain and for mutual profit and protection.[26]

Narratives of Friendship. More even than these occasional references to and statements about friendship, however, two biblical narratives that tell of the friendship of the principal characters merit closer attention as foundations for the view of friendship underlying the Fourth Gospel. As a part of Israel's scriptural heritage, the story of David and Jonathan told in 1 and 2 Samuel and the story of Ruth and Naomi that fills the book of Ruth would certainly have been familiar and precious to a Jewish community such as that to which the Fourth Gospel was written. Both explore how "friendship" does not depend on the traditional or legal bonds of kinship, but rather should manifest the same חסד ("covenant faithfulness") that defines God's relationship to Israel.

We are made aware of the friendship of David and Jonathan when the narrator informs us that their very lives are bound together: "The life (נפש) of Jonathan was bound to the life of David, and Jonathan loved him as he loved his own life" (1 Sam. 18:1, author's translation). This deep love becomes the basis of a covenant between them (1 Sam. 18:3), which sets in motion the interplay of political treason, personal loyalty, revenge, and grace that describes the transition from the reign of the house of Saul to that of the house of David. Despite occasional words that reflect the negative view of Israel's monarchy that was one thread in the tapestry of exilic assessments of Israel's history, the voice that prevails in this saga features two royal heroes, the king's son Jonathan and the future king David.

Saul's behavior is another story. His growing envy and ultimate hatred of the young David, whose military success and popular acclaim far outstrip any the king can claim, force Saul's son Jonathan to decide whether to betray his father to save his friend, or to desert his friend out of family loyalty. Jonathan opts for friendship, but seeks to build in protection for his descendants even while siding with David against Saul (1 Sam. 20:14–17, 42). Later, after Saul and his sons are killed in a battle with the Philistines (1 Sam. 38:1), King David has to conquer his desire for revenge against the house of Saul for all the years Saul had plotted his undoing, and he has to find within himself the grace to live out his covenant with Jonathan. The saga of enmity between the two houses ends in 2 Samuel 9:1, when David asks, "Is there still anyone left of the house of Saul to whom I may show covenant loyalty (חסד) for Jonathan's sake?" (author's translation), and welcomes Jonathan's remaining son into the royal household.

"Covenant faithfulness" (חסד) defines the friendship of David and Jonathan, a relationship that has personal, political, and theological dimensions. At the outset,

Jonathan as the king's son holds more power than David, but his defense of David against the wrath of Saul sets in motion a reversal of their relative power: "Jonathan knows that loyalty to David is not simply to a friend, but to one who will be king instead of him, and he asks of David loyalty as a king and not just as a friend."[27] Their fidelity to one another is understood as instrumental to the fulfillment of God's will expressed in the inauguration of David's reign, the initial point in the locus of God's new covenant with Israel. In fact, their fidelity to one another mirrors God's own covenant faithfulness, which is "both the attitude and the action of loyalty in relationships."[28] It includes extending deliverance or protection in order not to betray the person with whom one is in relationship, especially when that is necessary to deliver him or her from the threat of physical death or the social death of an end to the family name. It even includes forgiveness and unexpected acts of kindness.[29] Theologically, חסד is key to the continuation of God's covenant with God's people, for it entails not just God's loyalty to covenant obligations, but God's free act of deliverance of God's people. Though a noun, חסד is active, relational, and enduring. It preserves and promotes life. Though the LXX customarily translates it as ἔλεος, not φιλία or ἀγάπη, its role in the narrative of David and Jonathan makes it a part of the vocabulary of love or friendship.[30] The story of covenant faithfulness between Jonathan and David forms an important part of the scriptural heritage of the Johannine community and thus serves to elaborate the terse language of love in John 15.

The word חסד also links the story of David and Jonathan to that of Ruth and Naomi, which provides another important example within scripture of a relationship that can be classified as friendship. When the story begins, these women are mother-in-law and daughter-in-law. With the death of the man who provided the connection between them, however, their familial responsibility ends. Instead of going their separate ways as custom would dictate, the women live out a saga of danger, struggle, and commitment that echoes, at many points, the writings on friendship of the Greek and Hellenistic philosophers.

The story, set in the time of the judges, intertwines concerns of ethnicity and gender. Naomi is identified as a Bethlehemite whose family had fled to Moab to escape a famine at home. They settled there and made their home—apparently peacefully—among Israel's traditional enemies. Naomi's "sweet" life (recognized even in her name) becomes "bitter" with the loss of her husband and two sons. She decides to return home, and tries to send her two daughters-in-law back to their "mother's house," where presumably they could be given new husbands and begin life again. Her precarious future as an older woman alone changes when only one of the younger women, Orpah, obeys Naomi's order, while Ruth accompanies her home to Bethlehem.

Several details locate the telling of this story in the time after the exile, despite its alleged earlier setting. First, the reference to the "mother's house," to which the younger women were to return, mirrors the prominent role women were playing in postexilic society through their leadership in the household.[31] Second, the story tells in microcosm Israel's saga of exile and subsequent return, after having made their lives, as well as their living, in a foreign setting. Finally, there is the issue of the foreign wives singled out as problematic for those focused on concerns of religious purity among the returned people (for example, Ezra 9–10; Neh. 10:30; 13:23–29).[32]

Against this background, the story unfolds as a women's story.[33] Whether that points to a woman as author or to origins among a community of women storytellers is a matter of speculation, but the women's perspective is nonetheless clear. In particular, this story is cast as Naomi's story, despite the traditional title of the book. Naomi's fate brackets the story of the relationship between the women and the decisions they make. Her losses of husband and sons introduce the story, and her restored security through Ruth's bearing of a son for her signals the conclusion (4:14–17a). The story as a whole is incorporated into the logic of the story of Israel's history by the identification of that child as the grandfather of David and by the genealogy with which the book ends (4:18–22). That incorporation into the macro-narrative, however, alters the point of view of the rest of the story, which focuses on the women's needs, their relationship, and their collaboration to make the laws of Israel work for their well-being. The blessing in this story, unlike many of the patriarchal narratives, is not that of descendants, but that of the women's solidarity and survival.[34]

The women's story is one of commitment, travel, adventure, and finally conspiracy together for their common well-being. Language of friendship is not used, especially if the derivation of the name רות is linked not to רעות ("friend, companion") but to רוה ("to water to saturation").[35] Friendship is present, though, in the deep sense of solidarity between Ruth and Naomi[36] that is the difference between death and life for these women. Ruth the Moabite—a quintessential foreigner—is identified in 1:8 and 3:10 as the bearer of חסד, "covenant faithfulness," which is at the heart of the story of David and Jonathan and which defines God's own nature in this book (1:8; 2:20) as well as elsewhere in the Hebrew Bible.

Several points of intersection between the book of Ruth and the Fourth Gospel also suggest themselves. For example, there is the perspective or point of view of women, which shapes the book of Ruth (at least until the concluding verses), and which brings into focus key points of the narrative of the Fourth Gospel.[37] The issues of foreignness and foreigners also play a role in both. The Johannine community is located in the Diaspora, struggling with how to remain faithful there, just as Naomi has done; and that community appears to have incorporated foreigners, not unlike Ruth. Like Ruth and Naomi, members of the Johannine community are struggling to understand the rules of their new context and to make the laws work for them. Commitment to one another beyond traditional family obligations binds the Johannine community and indeed makes their community sustainable, just as it did for Ruth and Naomi. In both, "covenant love" is the foundation of their sense of God and of the work of the "redeemer" (גאל). In the book of Ruth, it is Boaz who plays that role, through the intervention of Ruth, and restores the family's parcel of land. In the Fourth Gospel the "redeemer" is Jesus, who "redeems," not a parcel of land, but the entire world (John 4:42).[38]

FRIENDSHIP ELABORATED:
EVIDENCE IN THE JOHANNINE NARRATIVE

This overview of aspects of friendship highlighted in both the biblical traditions of the Johannine community and the philosophical discussions of the Hellenistic world suggests a number of motifs by which friendship is elaborated in the Fourth Gospel, even when the language of friendship itself is absent. These motifs fall into two clusters. The first relates to friendship as a factor of daily life; the second relates to the role of friendship in situations of crisis or risk. The two categories are not always neatly divided in the Fourth Gospel. This is to be expected in the literature of a community who perceived that they faced the threat of rejection by their parent religious community as a final step of alienation following a fairly recent dislocation into the Diaspora—perhaps even within the memory of some in the community. These motifs of friendship, like the key passage of John 15:12–17, convey dimensions of the community's confession of Jesus' identity and his way of fulfilling the role of God's Anointed. At the same time motifs of friendship delineate the life of discipleship to which the community knew itself to be called.

Friendship and Daily Life

The declaration and commandments of friendship in John 15 have been prepared by the model of Jesus' daily engagement with and accompaniment of the community of followers. That he shares a common human condition with them is affirmed theologically in the statement, "The word became flesh and camped among us" (1:14, author's translation). Although the verb ἐσκήνωσεν already suggests what will subsequently be affirmed explicitly—namely, that Jesus' home in the sense of his origin and destination is elsewhere (see, for example, 8:12–59 and frequent references in John 13–17)—for the present he is "sent" from that place to live among them (1:11; 3:16–17, 34; 4:34; 5:24, 30, 36–38; 6:29, 38, 39, 44, 57; and passim).

A Ministry of Accompaniment. During his "encampment" with them, Jesus shares their lot and daily lives, relating to family, strangers, the curious, and the hostile as well as to his own community of associates. He is not separate from them, but in fact he knows them so well that at times he dares not "entrust himself to them" when danger threatens (2:23–25). Usually, though, he faces with them what they experience as the hostility of religious authorities. For example, when his healings place the healed person in jeopardy (as in the confrontations with authorities in John 5 and 9), Jesus is described as lingering or returning for additional conversations with the person who was healed. These extended stories are unlike the "hit-and-run" pattern of healing stories in the Synoptic Gospels, where Jesus does the healing and goes on his way. The further contact portrayed in the Fourth Gospel exposes Jesus to confrontation with and jeopardy from hostile accusers that is even greater than what is faced by the persons healed (5:14–47; 9:35–10:21). The word indeed was becoming flesh with them!

These bold actions by Jesus mirror the travails of "friends" in the stories philosophers used to tell—stories that define friendship in ways that concepts and propositions cannot. Jesus' actions also prefigure the accompaniment by the "other Paraclete" in the Christian community to whom the Gospel is directed (15:26–16:4; see chap. 6, below). This pattern of friendship thus characterizes the Fourth Gospel's description of Jesus and sets the agenda for life in the Christian community. Those whom Jesus accompanies in his life in the "flesh" become the new embodiment of accompaniment through the "other" who will follow when Jesus has returned to the one who sent him—and so the life of friendship continues.

A Verb with Staying Power. A powerful expression of the importance of the consistent and persistent presence that friendship entails for the Fourth Gospel can be found in the verb μένω. That verb is like a red thread running through the Fourth Gospel from beginning to end,[39] but its presence is masked by translators who render it by a variety of words, such as "live," "dwell," "remain," or "abide." The word μένω begins in John 1, where the question is where Jesus is "staying" (1:38, 39). It appears again in the request of the Samaritans who have come to believe (4:40). It figures in various notes about Jesus' travel plans (2:12; 7:9; 10:40; 11:6, 54). Wherever it occurs, that word traces the locus of Jesus' presence with those who receive him and, in an ironic twist, reminds them that he will not always be with them (14:25). But the word stretches beyond that common referent to express divine presence and, in the process, affirms the same about Jesus' sojourn. As a result, the simple questions of John 1:38— "τί ζητεῖτε;" and "ποῦ μένεις;"—become the key questions of discipleship for the church, namely, how to live out one's relationship with God.[40]

The word μένω is used in the LXX to convey divine "abiding" in such references as Daniel 6:26 and Psalms 9:7; 101:12. The heavenly council "abides," according to Isaiah 14:24, and so do other manifestations of God's presence—God's will, word, righteousness, and promised new creation, according to Psalms 32:11; 111:3, 9; Isaiah 40:8 and 66:2.[41] With that background, it is not surprising to find it used in the Fourth Gospel to express the abiding of the Holy Spirit (1:32, 33), God's word (5:38), and food that remains "for eternal life" (6:27). Most important, it conveys the mutual indwelling of God, Jesus, and those united to them (for example, 6:56; 14:10–11, 17; 15:4–7, 9–10). That unity depends on a constant flow of energy that has its origin in God. The disciples' ability to live out of that unity is rooted, not in their own moral excellence (obeying the commandment to love one another), but in the mutual love of God and Jesus (15:9–12). The relationship of mutual indwelling conveyed by the verb μένω emphasizes the permanence of that relationship (as conveyed in the comparison of the situation of the son and the slave in 8:35 and in the common expectation about the Messiah in 12:32) and of the blessings it conveys (for example, 12:46; 15:16). Thus, like Wisdom of whom it is said, "while remaining in herself, she renews all things; in every generation she passes into holy souls and makes them friends of God, and prophets" (Wisd. Sol. 7:27), Jesus' inviolable intimacy with God transforms his followers with the gift of a parallel relationship.[42] As Ernst Käsemann concludes, "Abiding with Jesus is possible only in the pilgrimage on that way which is Jesus himself."[43]

Sharing Meals. A particular aspect of daily life that is crucial to the maintenance of friendship is the sharing of meals. The theme of meals—be it the scandal of Jesus' table companions (for example, Matt. 9:11//Mark 2:16//Luke 5:30; Luke 15:2), the occasion of recognition of the risen Christ (Luke 24:30–31, 41–42), the normal practice of the gathered community (1 Cor. 11:17–22), or the specific commemoration of Jesus' last meal with his followers (1 Cor. 11:23–26; Matt. 26:26–29//Mark 14:22–25//Luke 22:15–20)—permeates the literature of the early church, including the Fourth Gospel. John shares with the Synoptic Gospels an account of Jesus' providing food for a multitude of people who had been following him (John 6:1–14; Matt. 14:13–21//Mark 6:32–44//Luke 9:10–17; Matt. 15:32–39//Mark 8:1–10). Its importance is reflected in its multiple attestation in the Gospels. In fact, it is the only event set in Jesus' public ministry narrated in all four Gospels. In the Fourth Gospel the event is called a σημεῖον, one of the series of events so identified because they point to the cross, the σημεῖον of Jesus' glorification and mediation of eternal life (3:14–15).[44] This event, especially with the discourse that follows, carries a rich variety of meanings in the theology of the Fourth Gospel. Many of these have been discussed in chapter 4 of this study, in the context of Jesus' identity as divine Wisdom. Here I will mention it only as an example of Jesus tending, as friends do, to the simple human need for food of those people gathered with him.

The Synoptic Gospels' references to Jesus' meals with unsavory table companions, by which those social outsiders become insiders, is not a theme of the Fourth Gospel. Rather, in this Gospel accounts of Jesus at meals mark the end of his time with his companions (12:2–8; 13:1–30), and the third appearance of the Risen One (21:1–14). The emphasis is thus on their importance for the life of the community, those especially identified as his friends. In other words, they reveal something about Jesus and about the continuity of the church. The meals at the end of Jesus' public ministry try again to prepare the community to understand and accept Jesus' death. The anointing of Jesus by Mary of Bethany constitutes, on one level, her act of welcome and hospitality to the friend and guest who has come to her home for dinner (12:2–3), and, on another level, it is interpreted as the loving work of preparing her friend for burial (12:7). Her wiping of his feet is echoed in Jesus' act at a subsequent supper, when he washed his followers' feet as an example of the servant form their own friendship is to take (13:12–20). The breakfast on the beach is another "miraculous" feeding that provides the disciples both nourishment and food for thought and understanding as they prepare to move from a time of memory of Jesus' time on earth into the new stage of the community's life. The friendship known in the shared meal, and in the commitment to one another that it expressed, extended to the time when the Gospel was written, and even beyond, as the discussion (below) of the dialogue between Jesus and Peter makes clear.

Friendship and Times of Crisis

The line between everyday life and occasions of crisis is not always clear. Sickness and death are facts of everyday life, yet to those who experience them themselves or in their families or communities, they are crises that can reorder one's physical circumstances, one's priorities, and one's relationships, and even threaten one's faith. At such moments the friendships that undergird daily life with presence and companionship can be the key to survival itself. Friends interrupt plans and schedules to respond as they are needed and able. They support, encourage, and help their friends who are in need wherever and whenever they can, regardless of the cost. So the philosophers tell us, and so we know from our own experience, if we are blessed with friends. The Fourth Gospel is permeated by specific examples in which Jesus lives out this dimension of friendship in times of crisis. The narrative of that Gospel is held together by the picture of Jesus as the one who commits his very life on behalf of his friends and who requires no less of them. In that way it proclaims his story as the "good news" that brings life to a community whose entire world seems to be hanging in the balance.

Caring in Sickness and Death. Illness and death are personal experiences with social implications. They appear to change the shape and meaning of all of one's surroundings. Friends, the philosophers say, care for one another in such times, and according to all four Gospels Jesus' care of those who were ill came to expression in his healing ministry. The expansion of the Fourth Gospel's accounts of healing through more sustained interaction and dialogue with those healed and with various bystanders makes healing in that Gospel an expression of friendship, as well as simply of Jesus' compassion or a special power. As noted earlier, when that extended contact places the healer himself in jeopardy (as in the stories in John 5 and 9), the help and care echo with even greater clarity the philosophers' stories that define friendship.

A special case of the link of friendship and care in times of illness can be seen in the story of the raising of Lazarus (11:1–44). There Jesus' "love" for Lazarus and his sisters (v. 3, where the verb is φιλέω, and v. 5, where it is ἀγαπάω) is the basis for much of their conversation, for the high emotional engagement attributed to Jesus, and for the interplay of expectations and surprises on which the plot turns. Knowing that Lazarus has died (v. 14), Jesus moves into the liminal space where death and life come together, and where only family members or close friends go. Like οἱ Ἰουδαῖοι, who in this instance also play the role of friends when they come to console the bereaved sisters (v. 19), Jesus spends time with them, listens to them, talks with them, and—as ordinary friends and comforters cannot do—restores Lazarus to life. In the process the hostility of the authorities against him is escalated, and his own arrest warrant is sealed (11:45–57).

As the account unfolds in John 11, Lazarus is said already to have been in the tomb when Jesus arrives, and Jesus' act is to call him from the tomb to the land of the living. Jesus therefore does not need to be involved in caring for and burying Lazarus's corpse, which was a duty that would have been accepted only by family members, by the disciples of a rabbi, or by the closest of friends. Though that dimension of friendship is not part of the account of Jesus and Lazarus, it is introduced at the end of the Gospel account, when Nicodemus and Joseph of Arimathea tend and bury Jesus' own body (19:38–42). Their act of friendship is even more dramatic in light of the political risk that might have been incurred by claiming the body of one executed by Rome, as Jesus was. Their tender and courageous act forms an appropriate closing parenthesis around a story where the daily rhythms of friendship mark both Jesus' identity and the life of the community of his followers.

Friends and Families. The Hellenistic philosophers whose works we have considered as background to the understanding of friendship in the Johannine community include the needs of a friend's family members—especially parents, spouses, or children—on a par with the friend's own circumstances. Friends take responsibility for each other's families and become, in effect, each other's new "families" of responsibility and commitment. This is particularly so in times of crisis when the usual patterns and mechanisms of support break down. The account of the wedding at Cana at the beginning of Jesus' ministry (2:1–11) and his touching words from the cross (19:26–27) frame the Gospel with just such examples.

The account of the wedding at Cana (2:1–11) is the first of the "signs" that set in motion the story of Jesus' journey to the cross. The symbolic development of the story as a replacement narrative, in which the water of Jewish purification rituals is replaced by the apparently superior "Christian" wine that Jesus gives, takes place in the framework of an account of a friend coming to the rescue of other friends in a crisis. I use the word "friends" because nothing is said about their being Jesus' kin. His action on their behalf thus amounts to his taking responsibility for the honor of the host family. The crisis is identified by Jesus' (unnamed) mother: The hosts will be shamed by the lack of sufficient wine for the party. Jesus' flamboyant resolution of the crisis—when a simple trip to the local merchant might have solved the problem—makes clear how far he will go to protect the honor of the hosts, even at the price of an action that, in the macro-narrative of the Gospel, leads toward his own death.[45]

It is the crisis of his death that initiates the second example of this expression of friendship (19:26–27). At the foot of the cross, along with his mother, her sister Mary (the wife of Clopas), and Mary Magdalene, there is one identified only as "the disciple whom he loved." This unnamed disciple repeatedly takes center stage in this Gospel, and it is this disciple's testimony that undergirds the Gospel (21:24). The presence of the beloved disciple in the Johannine narrative appears to supplement the tradition that locates the various women at that place of horror and intimacy, and thus to highlight that disciple's importance.[46] Jesus' dying word commends his mother and the beloved disciple to each other's care; they become mother and "child" to each other. The Greek word is υἱός, which can refer either to a male offspring or to a child whose sex is not identified. Church tradition and critical scholarship concur in assuming this disciple to be a male. Indeed, as the philosopher's narratives about the actions of friends corroborate, in the Hellenistic world a son would have the responsibility to protect and care for the mother of the family, and a son would appropriately seek a substitute if he could not discharge that responsibility himself. It is not inherently impossible, however, for a daughter or even a daughter-in-law to take on such responsibility, as the book of Ruth bears witness. Given that two of the three members of the family of Bethany—the only characters in the Gospel explicitly identified as "loved" by Jesus—are women, and given the significant roles played by women in the narrative of the Fourth Gospel (especially the Samaritan woman in chap. 4, Mary and

Martha in chaps. 11 and 12, and Mary Magdalene in chap. 20), this friend who shared the literary and historical fate of many women whose names have been lost or hidden might in fact have been commissioned as his mother's (female) "child" in the new community catalyzed by Jesus' "glorification."

The "Good"[47] *Shepherd.* Another image of friendship that draws on the consistent presence, care, and nurture demonstrated to friends in the rhythms of daily life, but that moves over into the realm of friendship in times of crisis, is the figure of the shepherd in 10:1–18. The figure of the shepherd is taken for granted by church tradition as a christological designation, if not a christological title in the usual sense of that term: Jesus is the Good Shepherd. The image is often romanticized, particularly through pictures of a well-scrubbed young man in a clean and freshly ironed white robe, standing in a rural setting reminiscent of the New England hills, and cuddling a baby lamb.[48] In popular interpretation the παροιμία (10:6) in John is usually conflated with the parable of the Synoptic tradition (specifically, in Q: Matt. 18:12–14//Luke 15:4–6). The result is that the details of John's image that point in the direction of friendship are ignored.

It is important to acknowledge at the outset one point in which the παροιμία does not fit with friendship, and that is the one-sidedness of the relationship of the shepherd and the sheep. The former is clearly the caregiver and the dominant partner. While it is true of friends that at a given moment one will shoulder the burden of care for the other, usually that is not a permanent state of affairs (or if it becomes permanent, as in a terminal illness, the friends usually share a history of greater mutuality). In the case of the shepherd and the sheep, however, one cannot envision a time when their situations would be reversed. Despite that obvious lack of the mutuality that usually marks a relationship of friendship, the description of the shepherd echoes several aspects of that relationship. In the nature of things, shepherds and sheep spend long hours together. That leads to a recognition that goes both ways: the sheep respond to the shepherd's voice, and the shepherd knows the sheep's names—or probably has actually given them names that highlight their uniqueness ("Old Curly-Horn," "Mrs. Black-Socks").[49] In contrast to the "thief and bandit" (10:1), the shepherd is reliable, honest, and straightforward.

The real test, though, comes at moments of crisis, when the sheep are threatened by marauders, whether human or animal. In the night, the time of greatest danger, the shepherd becomes the gate to the sheep's pen (10:7–10), lying down across the opening as a barrier to all danger.[50] Like friends (15:13), shepherds "appoint"—or, in this case, literally "lay down"—their lives for those entrusted to them (10:11; the verb again is τίθημι). Raymond Brown argues that because in the Fourth Gospel that verb clearly refers to Jesus' death, the language is inappropriate in this context.[51] I would suggest that the argument goes in the opposite direction. That is, this παροιμία of the model shepherd, which precedes the reference in 15:13 that is taken as definitive for the word τίθημι, establishes its meaning. While the purpose of the shepherd is to safeguard the life of the sheep even at the risk of his (?) own life, the intent is that the shepherd be alive in the morning! Similarly, the point of the standard of friendship is that the friend be prepared to risk his or her life on behalf of a friend, but life and not death is the purpose.[52] The challenge this poses to traditional christological thought is that it suggests that the author of the Fourth Gospel may not have viewed Jesus' death as the intended or necessary outcome. Rather, the purpose is "life" (10:10), and to this end, Jesus commits his whole life, even, if necessary, to the point of death. In that sense, he is the "model" shepherd, just as in 15:12–17 he is the friend who both commands friendship and makes it possible.

Jesus' identity as the "model shepherd" is portrayed in action in 20:11–18.[53] The occasion is set at a moment of crisis for the disciples who have not yet experienced Jesus' resurrection. The first part of the chapter deals with the disciples' concern over the fate and location of Jesus' body. Mary Magdalene is portrayed as still pursuing that question in her parallel conversations with the angels in verse 13 and the "gardener" in verse 15. She has physically "turned around" (ἐπιστράφη εἰς τὰ ὀπίσω) in verse 14 to face the latter new arrival. Her crucial "turning" in verse 16 has no complement, and it should be seen as depicting her (inner) reorientation away from "the things that lie behind" and toward the future shaped by her recognition of the risen Christ.[54] That turning is evoked when she hears him call her name. The voice of the risen one (in v. 15) has not been sufficient by itself, but that voice calling her by name (10:3) allows her, in turn, to recognize him as the teacher (Ραββουνί) who can direct her toward her new role in the community shaped by the truth of the resurrection. The role of the symbol of the broken bread "opening the eyes" of the disciples on the road to Emmaus (Luke 24:31) is played here by the "model shepherd." Both symbolic narratives are pictured as at once the catalyst and the content of the subsequent resurrection message proclaimed to the other followers (John 20:18; Luke 24:35). In the Fourth Gospel Jesus' role as the good shepherd embroiders the motif of friendship developed in 15:12–17 as a metaphor for both Jesus' identity and the life of the post-Easter community.

Shepherding the Community. The episode with Mary Magdalene in 20:11–18 establishes the importance of Jesus' "shepherding" friendship with "his own" in their ability to embrace the reality of his resurrection. In the dialogue with Peter in 21:15–17, the same motif becomes constitutive of the practice of leadership in the community. Peter comes as a bit of a surprise in this narrative of a dialogue with the risen Christ; one might anticipate finding instead the unnamed "disciple whom Jesus loved." Between the account of the call of the disciples in chapter 1 and the passion narrative, Peter appears only twice (6:6, 68). Only the latter of these, when he responds to Jesus with the confession, "You have the words of eternal life," hints at a significant role in defining the faith or practice of the community. His misunderstanding of Jesus' action of foot washing (13:6–10) and his subsequent triple denial of Jesus (13:36–37; 18:15–27) do little to lead one to anticipate such an account in the final chapter of the Gospel.

Apparently, however, the Johannine community was aware of traditions in other parts of the early church that accorded Peter a central role. His presence in the foot race to the tomb with the beloved disciple (20:1–10) and in the Easter episode by the Sea of Tiberias (John 21) suggests a willingness to grant that role a narrative place in the Fourth Gospel, albeit one that expresses his importance in terms consistent with that community's way of viewing the church.

Several details accomplish that project. First, Peter's earlier confession about the power of Jesus' words (6:68) is confronted by the pattern of repeated questions that show Peter not recognizing the locus of life in the question about his "love" for Jesus. Here as elsewhere in the Fourth Gospel, the verbs φιλέω and ἀγαπάω function as synonyms. The problem is not that Peter uses the incorrect verb in his answer, but that he does not recall that to love Jesus means to keep his command-ment (14:15), which is that they love one another as he has loved them (15:12). Three times he has an opportunity to undo his earlier denials, and each time he stops short. His answers remain incomplete because they never extend to include love—appointing his life—for the others, but remain focused on Jesus.[55] Whether that correction of Peter was intended to address what the author perceives as the christocentric excess (while ignoring the community) in sectors of the early church identified with Peter's leadership, or whether it was intended as a warning against such tendencies in the Johannine community itself, is impossible to know. In any event, the terms by which that love is elaborated recall the παροιμία of John 10.[56] Love for Jesus, expressed in love for one another, takes the form of faithful shep-herding. Jesus was *the* model shepherd, but others now must carry on the shep-herd's task. It appears significant that neither Peter nor anyone else is called "another shepherd." The noun applied to others might risk becoming a title, and this author seems to eschew titles, especially for leaders in the church. Just as peo-ple are "sent" but not called ἀπόστολοι, Peter is assigned the tasks without the ti-tle of "shepherd." Presumably the tasks are not reserved to him, in some sort of apostolic primacy, but he too must fulfill them. In this matter of shepherding, as will be shown again in the discussion of the "other παράκλητος" (in chap. 6, be-low), according to the Fourth Gospel the church is the place where the ministry in-carnated in Jesus, and especially the ministry of friendship in all of its manifestations, is a word "become flesh" anew in each generation.

CONCLUSION

With the image of the model shepherd, this discussion of friendship in the Fourth Gospel comes full circle. The shepherd's patient spending of time with the sheep—sharing the circumstances of their daily life, nurturing and caring for them, coming to know them by name, and, if necessary, risking his very life on their be-half—is the life of a friend among friends. That picture summarizes in vivid col-ors not only the sayings about friendship in 15:12–17, but also the three-year saga of the daily rhythms of friendship and the stunning examples of solidarity in mo-ments of crisis that are portrayed in the Gospel narrative. Throughout that narra-tive Jesus "appoints" his life on behalf of those he calls his "friends." In doing that he also fulfills the commission for which he has been sent, namely, to embody God's love for "the world" (3:16). He is the friend who befriends others, and in the process he teaches them how to be friends to one another in the community of his followers, both while he "encamps" with them (1:14) and after his "glorifica-tion" and resurrection. Jesus is portrayed as the model friend who does not desert his friends in the face of hostility, and the model shepherd whose body becomes the door protecting the sheep from harm. His friendship unites his followers with himself, and with God who sent him, in an indestructible bond that is life itself. His challenge to Peter and his "commandment" that the disciples show their love for him by their love for one another ("appointing" their lives on one another's behalf) describe the call that constitutes and shapes the Christian community. This image of the church emphasizes actions rather than roles as definitive of its identity, namely, that its members so commit their lives to one another that no risk is too great to take on behalf of the life and well-being of these friends.

In the Fourth Gospel, then, friendship is related as much to ecclesiology as to Christology—or perhaps for the Fourth Gospel it is ecclesiological because it is christological. The verb in that designation is sometimes ἀγαπάω and sometimes φιλέω, but the phenomenon is clearly friendship, and it is on the authority of that experience and relationship in the life of the "disciple whom Jesus loved" that the story contained in the Gospel is told and believed (21:24). Both the gift and the demand of the church is that its members be friends in this serious way, so that the Gospel story and the life that it conveys can go on.

Chapter 6

The "Other Paraclete":
The Story Continues

The body of the Gospel provides ample evidence that the author views the man Jesus as incarnation of the λόγος and thus, by extension, of Wisdom. Wisdom's preexistent co-creative work with God is carried forward in his story of love for and commitment to his followers, his rejection by "his own," his efforts to mediate the "way" of life, and the hospitality, friendship, and accompaniment of those connected to him in the covenant of divine love and human responsibility. That very move of Wisdom into the concreteness of a specific human life introduced a new set of problems, however, when that person died. Would Jesus' followers be left with nothing more than memories of the past and rules for the future? Had Wisdom abandoned the yearning for a dwelling place among humankind, and—as in the writings of Philo and in *1 Enoch* and *2 Esdras*—taken refuge again in the heavenly regions whence she came? The various sayings about Jesus' origins from God (or "above") and his need to return there to prepare a place for his followers (3:13; 8:21–23; 14:2–3, 28–30) suggest precisely that: The resurrected Christ dwells with God. Following a few post-Easter appearances to his immediate followers, he would be seen no longer on earth. The locus of promise is not a creation transformed into a fitting home for Wisdom, but—for followers of the Word—redemption to another eternal home.

The early church wrestled with various solutions to the potential pastoral problem raised by Jesus' death and evident absence, and by the temporally or geographically deferred hope. Belief in and eager awaiting of Christ's return in glory for a final event of judgment and ultimate triumph for the "righteous" or the "believers" was apparently the most common expression of this hope in the early church. With that hope focused on the future went affirmations that, in the interim, the Holy Spirit would remain with the believers and animate the church with God's continuing presence. The Fourth Gospel carried a different version of that word of assurance. It focused on the promise of the divine gift of the παράκλητος in whom divine Wisdom will find her new dwelling place on earth once Jesus has departed.[1]

Because the term itself is unusual, the starting point for our study of the meaning of that promise must be a study of the nuances and history of the word. With that background we can examine what is claimed about this figure in the Fourth Gospel. That picture is then contextualized in the larger narrative context of the christological and ecclesiological project of the Fourth Gospel.

The word παράκλητος is related to the verb παρακαλέω, literally, "to call alongside" or "summon," but occasionally with the derivative meaning "comfort."[2] The use of the noun is attested in secular Greek as early as the fourth century B.C.E. to refer to a person called to give assistance. The word seems connected to legal contexts, though it is not a technical term for a court official.[3] Except for two manuscripts that use the word to identify the friends otherwise recognized as "comforters" of Job 16:2, the noun does not occur in the Septuagint. Its use there may reflect the use in the LXX of the verb παρακαλέω to render the Hebrew נחם, "comfort" or "console." The meaning "comforter" for the noun deviates, however, from the usual meaning of "advocate" that the word retains in Philo, in early Christian literature outside the New Testament, and where it occurs as a loan-word in rabbinic texts.[4] The word is found in the New Testament only in John 14:16, 26; 15:26; 16:7 and in the closely related 1 John 2:1. The basic meaning of "advocate" is reflected in 1 John 2:1, where Christ is portrayed as an advocate with God on behalf of sinful believers.

That background would lead one to propose the meaning of "advocate" where the word is used in the Fourth Gospel (as is the case in the New Revised Standard Version, Jerusalem Bible, New English Bible, and Revised English Bible), but the history of interpretation and translation has not always supported that choice. Two factors account for the resulting range of translations. First, in the Gospel the term does not carry the intercessory meaning found in 1 John. Instead, the work of the παράκλητος in the Fourth Gospel is directed toward the believers themselves, or through them toward the hostile world. Second, since the term occurs only in the speech attributed to Jesus on the night of his arrest, and since the principal theme of the speech is the preparation of Jesus' followers to deal with his approaching absence, a number of translators have chosen to direct the meaning of the word toward their pastoral needs ("Comforter" [King James Version], "Counselor" [Revised Standard Version], "Helper" [Today's English Version and New Revised Standard Version note], "*Consolador*" [Reina Valera]).[5] An examination of the passages where the term occurs is necessary in order to clarify its meaning in the Fourth Gospel.

THE WORD παράκλητος IN ITS LITERARY CONTEXT IN THE FOURTH GOSPEL

The four occurrences of the terms in the Fourth Gospel are in Jesus' address to his disciples on the night of his address (John 13–17). That farewell discourse is a complex tapestry of themes, the various threads of which surface and disappear again in intricate patterns and designs. One's conclusion about the dominant pattern depends on the limits of the section identified for study—how close or how far away one has focused the zoom lens of one's investigative camera. Small sections exhibit their own structure, but then when the view broadens, parts of the smaller sections turn out to play roles in the larger design in which they partici-pate.[6] This complexity doubtless stems from the interweaving of source materi-als and their subsequent redactions, through a lengthy process of the Gospel's formation.

For the purposes of this study, the four occurrences of the term παράκλητος es-tablish the dimensions of the text being examined. The resulting "unit," then, is 14:15–16:15. That unit exhibits the following structure:

A. 14:15–26—First Paraclete Section: Love, Commandment, Presence

B. 14:27–31—Jesus' Leave-taking: Assurance for the Community

C. 15:1–17—Friendship and Accompaniment

B'. 15:18–25 [16:2–3]—Jesus' Leave-taking: Threat from "the World"

A'. 15:26–16:15—Second Paraclete Section: Testimony against "the World"

The two sections in which the Paraclete is named set forth that figure's threefold task as providing the believers with assurance of divine presence and peace, teach-ing the believers and guiding them into truth, and enabling the believers to testify to the world about Jesus.[7] These sections frame and thus define a reflection on how Jesus' followers (and their followers who read this Gospel) are to continue and fur-ther Jesus' "works" after he returns to God who sent him (14:12). The challenge these followers face has two dimensions: their own grief, both at the loss of a friend and companion and at their awareness of all that they still do not understand; and their experience of the hostility of "the world" (15:18–25) and, in particular, of religious authorities (16:2), which they understand to be a consequence of their discipleship.

DETAILED ANALYSIS: THE παράκλητος IN THE CHRISTOLOGY AND ECCLESIOLOGY OF THE FOURTH GOSPEL

An examination of the passages that speak of the παράκλητος provide an ap-propriate lens through which to examine the relationship of that figure to the Gospel's portrait of Jesus and to the company of Jesus' followers after his death, resurrection, and return to his place of origin with God.

The First Paraclete Section:
Love, Commandment, Presence (14:15–26)

The passage that introduces the Paraclete in the Fourth Gospel is itself in the shape of a chiasmus, as follows:

a. 14:15–18—The Paraclete, the Spirit of Truth: receive, abide, know

b. 14:19–21—Love and keeping commandments

c. 14:22—Distinction between disciples and world: reveal

b'. 14:23–24—Love and keeping "words"

a'. 14:25–26—The Paraclete, the Holy Spirit: teach, remind

The section is introduced by a saying that links loving Jesus and keeping his "commandments." The problem, apparently introduced by the plural form even though this Gospel attributes only one commandment to Jesus (13:34; 15:12), fades in light of the striking parallels between this commandment of Jesus in John and Deuteronomy 5:10; 7:9; and 11:1, where, in the context of Moses' farewell discourse, loving God also is associated with keeping "the commandments" (plural).[8] Just as the reference in Deuteronomy is to the entire instruction or Torah seen as a whole, so for the writer of the Fourth Gospel the commandment that they are to love one another following the model of Jesus' love for them summarizes the instruction or "way" of Jesus.

The combination of the motifs of love and keeping commandments occurs with various pairs of subjects and objects in 14:21, 23, 24, 31; 15:10, 12. In 14:15, however, these motifs serve as the protasis and the first half of a compound apodosis setting forth a covenant between the disciples and the soon-to-be-departing Jesus, who makes a commitment on God's behalf. That covenant introduces the παράκλητος, further identified as ἄλλος παράκλητος, "another Paraclete," which suggests that there has been a prior one. The context of the preparation for Jesus' absence posits him as the prototype, and the claims made about this "other's" role confirm that identification.[9]

The parallels between Jesus and the Paraclete are striking. The link between the two figures is made explicit by the first-person singular verbs in 14:18: The one who is speaking and the promised one who is coming speak with a single voice. Furthermore, a number of passages set out parallel features of the two figures. Both are emissaries sent from God (3:16, 17; 5:24, 30, 36; 7:28; 8:16, 29; 12:44, 45, 49; 14:16, 26), and both come into the world from a place of origin with God (5:43; 15:26; 16:7, 13, 28; 18:37). Like the Word made flesh, the Paraclete is neither recognized nor received by the world (1:11–13; 5:53; 8:19; 10:14; 12:48; 14:7, 17, 19; 16:3, 16–17), but only by those to whom the Sender grants it. Each speaks not of self but of what is heard (7:17; 8:26–28; 14:10; 16:13). Both Jesus and the Paraclete are identified with "the truth" (8:32; 14:6, 17; 15:26; 16:13; 18:37).[10] Both teach (7:14–15; 8:20; 14:26; 18:19); give testimony (5:31–38; 7:7; 8:13–18; 15:26); reveal, disclose, and proclaim (4:25; 16:13–15, 25); and convict the world (3:19–20; 9:41; 15:22; 16:8).[11]

As this list of common features makes clear, just as personified Wisdom forms a significant part of the background for the Johannine Jesus, it also offers background for the Paraclete (see Wisd. Sol. 9:11; 10:10; Sir. 24:12, 26–27, 33; 1 Enoch 42:2).[12] In addition to these common features in the Fourth Gospel, the Wisdom of Solomon provides a precedent for connecting Wisdom and the Holy Spirit, in that the two are equated in their functions and in their role of mediation between God and humankind (Wisd. Sol. 1:4–6, 9; 9:17–18).[13] With this promise of the Paraclete as another expression of Wisdom's presence, even

Jesus' crucifixion does not force the author to share the pessimistic conclusion of *1 Enoch* and *2 Esdras* that Wisdom must be confined to the heavenly places because she has been rejected on earth. Instead, she has a new dwelling place on earth, even while returning to be with God.[14]

Verse 18 gives another important clue to the identity and function of this one who is to come. That clue links the ἄλλος παράκλητος to the motif of friendship that we have already seen connected to the Fourth Gospel's proclamation of Jesus. The assurance that the disciples will not be left "orphans" (ὀρφανούς) applies to them a term common in the LXX (most frequently in commandments about protecting "widows and orphans"), but occurring only twice in the New Testament. James 1:27 clearly parallels the LXX usage and appears to refer to the community's responsibility for these potentially most vulnerable members of the society. Here, however, the term is applied to Jesus' followers, whose apprehension at being left alone in the world is suggested narratively by Peter's request to follow Jesus (13:37), Thomas's ignorance about where he was going (14:5), and Philip's request to see God (14:8). This description of the disciples as "orphans" resembles the use of that term to refer to the experience of students bereft of their teacher among the Greek philosophers.[15] In both cases, the emotional sorrow is secondary to the vulnerability resulting from the loss of a guiding force and advocate that is an aspect of their bereavement. Those left behind need someone to provide comfort in the form of presence and assurance that they are not alone, and they need someone who can advise them and represent them in their interaction with others. The relationship of presence and advocacy that they have experienced with Jesus prior to his departure resulted from Jesus' "abiding" (μένω) with them. That relationship of friendship or accompaniment (discussed relative to the portrait of Jesus in chap. 5, above) is now carried forward by the presence of this "other" who is just like him (1:38, 39; 2:12; 4:40; 6:56; 11:54; 12:46; 14:10, 17, 25; 15:4, 5, 6, 7, 9, 10, 16).

This dimension of the assurance provided in the promise of the Paraclete needs to be linked also with 19:26, where the dying Jesus confides "the disciple whom he loved" and his own mother into each other's care, in what is a classical expression of friendship. Both are thus saved from potential vulnerability when Jesus will no longer be with them. They are not left "orphaned." Nothing is said about the Holy Spirit or the παράκλητος, but rather they are to provide that assurance for one another. I think that apparent omission is no coincidence. In the narrative sequence, the scene at the cross recalls the promised assurance of the farewell discourse. When the Gospel is reread by the community, the discourse invokes that touching scene, and in the process conveys an important theological point linking the Paraclete to Jesus. Just as the λόγος "became flesh" in the man Jesus, and in that form both embodied divine Wisdom and befriended "his own," so the ἄλλος παράκλητος too is not an amorphous spirit-presence, but rather is known to them embodied in other members of the community.[16]

The second step of the chiasmus, 14:19–21, develops the assurance of accompaniment that stretches into the future. Key to that assurance is the "knot" of mutual indwelling that integrates Jesus, God, and the disciples (v. 20), and that is linked to their participation in "love" for one another (v. 21).[17] Against our modern association of love only with an emotional connection, or perhaps to the practice of friendship hinted in the previous section, here love is connected to Wisdom themes. Love is linked to their knowledge of Jesus (v. 20) and his self-revelation to them (v. 21), which will be among the tools equipping them for life in the time when the Jesus they have known is absent. The temporal perspective of the entire discourse, and in particular this section, is telescopic, in that the assurance allegedly to Jesus' immediate followers encompasses as well the readers and hearers of the Gospel in subsequent generations. The reason is that the Jesus whom the first disciples *had* known is the same who *is* and *will be* known to subsequent generations in the "other" form of the Paraclete.

The "hinge" or pivot point of this initial smaller chiasmus, verse 22, underlines the separation between the disciples and "the world" which had already been introduced in verse 17, and which will be developed in 15:18–25. It is that distinction, which moves into separation and finally opposition, that underlies their vulnerability as "orphans" and the necessity for this abiding Advocate.

The chiasmus is completed in two stages. The first takes up again the interrelationship of love and commandment (now called Jesus' "word" given to him from God), and the consequence of divine presence, in verses 23–24. That first step of the chiasmus is then echoed in verses 25–26, where the Paraclete is now identified as the Holy Spirit instead of, as earlier, the Spirit of Truth. Once again the motif of agency is present,[18] as the Spirit is identified as sent by God in Christ's name, and once again the Paraclete has the task of teaching (as also in 16:13), and specifically of reminding them of what Jesus has already taught.

Jesus' Leave-taking: Assurance for the Community (14:27–31)

The repetitiveness of themes in the "farewell discourse" of the Fourth Gospel is too obvious to require argument. That repetitiveness has led many scholars to suggest that this portion of the Gospel (as well as perhaps larger sections or the Gospel as a whole) has undergone several redactions, as the community reflected in a variety of contexts on the implications of these treasured accounts of words said to be Jesus' final message before his death. The last clause of 14:31 ("rise, let us be on our way") suggests that at one stage of its development the discourse ended here. The verses that come between the second mention of the Paraclete (in v. 26) and this conclusion (in v. 31c) fit with such a narrative context. They focus on Jesus' leave-taking with an emphasis on assurance for the disciples about the desirability of this departure for him (his return to his place of origin with God) and them ("peace I leave with you"). This section draws the hearers in, toward a center that is solid and reliable. God's own faithfulness is affirmed as sufficient for Jesus and for them—an assurance that will stand in sharper relief when the threat against the community from "the world" is identified in the parallel section on Jesus' leave-taking in 15:18–25.

Friendship and Accompaniment (15:1–17)

Between the two sections that focus on Jesus' leave-taking (14:27–31 and 15:18–25) is the central section (15:1–17) of the larger chiasmus that shapes the portion of the Gospel we are examining. (It is discussed in detail in chapter 5, and that discussion will be only summarized here.) It begins with the image of the vine as a figure for the nature and meaning of the relationship between Jesus and his hearers (15:1–11). Themes of love, abiding (μένω), and keeping the commandments are elaborated upon in this reflection that echoes and develops sayings of 14:15–26. Verses 12–17 examine even more closely the nature of Jesus' commandment (13:34; 14:15, 21, 23, 24) and link it to "friendship" as the relationship of Jesus to the disciples, and of them to one another.

As the climactic point of the "hinge" of the chiasmus within which John's discussion of the ἄλλος παράκλητος is inscribed, 15:12–17 portrays Jesus as one who befriends and calls the followers to be friends of one another and thereby establishes a crucial dimension of the work of this parallel figure who is to come. The Paraclete will continue to enable friendship to be the lifestyle of the community, which sustains them and establishes a mode of divine presence in their midst. This presence not only provides comfort and strength for the community from within, but also equips the community as it interfaces with a hostile world (15:18–25; 16:2–3). This "world," in turn, sets the context for the role of the Paraclete set forth in the final section of the chiasmus (15:26–16:15).

Jesus' Leave-taking from "the World" (15:18–25 [16:2–3])

Warnings about the world's opposition to Jesus have been expressed earlier in the Fourth Gospel (7:7), but there the community was explicitly exempted from that hatred. Now they are warned that they too will be its objects if they continue to embody the divine presence as he did, which is precisely what they have been assured will be the case (15:12–17). The world's responsibility for that hatred is linked to their refusal to receive Jesus (a recurring theme since 1:11), just as they also refuse to accept the "other Paraclete" (14:17). The general opposition of "the world" is given sharper focus in 16:2–3, which repeats the threat that they will be declared ἀποσυνάγωγοι (9:22; 12:42). This dire forecast of what lies ahead for the disciples, which presumably the Johannine community would recognize as a depiction of their reality, requires brief elaboration.

The Second Paraclete Section: Testimony against "the World" (15:26–16:15)

The second introduction of the Paraclete (15:26–16:15) responds to the hostile context sketched in 15:18–25 and 16:2–3 by accentuating the "advocacy" role of the παράκλητος, who is again called also "the Spirit of truth." In that role the Paraclete both provides direct testimony (15:26) and sustains the members of the community when they themselves must testify concerning the one in whom they believe (15:27). The specific foci of the Paraclete's own testimony are spelled out in 16:8–11, and 16:12–15 addresses the continuing task of the Spirit of truth to instruct them in—or, more precisely, lead them into—"all the truth" (16:13). The section as a whole forms yet another chiasmus, as follows:

a. 15:26–16:1—"Testimony" of the Paraclete and the community: to keep them from stumbling

b. 16:2–4a—Opposition from the synagogue: so that they remember

b'. 16:4b–7—Jesus' departure: so that the Paraclete will be sent

a'. 16:8–15—"Testimony" of the Paraclete: to convict the world and to guide the community into "all the truth"

Despite the courtroom language and tone of this section, no formal arena of defense is described. Instead, the assumption is that the disciples, and by implication the Johannine community, like John the Baptist (1:15, 32) and those who met Jesus (4:39, 12:17) before them, must become witnesses to Jesus in their own context.

The Paraclete is crucial to the ongoing instruction that is necessary as the time since Jesus' own teaching grows longer, and as the specific circumstances in which the testimony is required change. The assumption is that the basic opposition between the vision or "way" (14:4–6) of Jesus and that of the world will continue, but that the case for the world's error needs to be made each generation afresh. The dynamic of continuity between Jesus and this one who is to come (emphasized in 16:7, where Jesus himself is the sender of whom the Paraclete is the agent, and not only the one in whose name God does the sending as in 14:26) and discontinuity of circumstances is conveyed by three temporal indicators in this section. First, we are reminded that those addressed have been with Jesus ἀπ' ἀρχῆς (15:27), and that is why they are called upon to testify. Second, Jesus' presence with them meant that he could not say ἐξ ἀρχῆς what his imminent departure now makes appropriate (16:4). A third moment is indicated when he will still (ἔτι) need to communicate more to them than they can bear at this moment (16:12), and they will be led into that full truth by the very Spirit of truth (16:13–14).

Section a of this chiasmus (15:26–16:1) provides no content to the Paraclete's testimony to the world. The author's perception of the hostile context in which the community finds itself, which is made evident in section b (16:2–4a), invokes another aspect of the background to this figure identified with the Spirit of truth. The Qumran literature (and possibly the *Testament of Judah* 20:1–5) provides the only known pre-Christian use of the latter title. There the figure appears sometimes as an angelic presence guiding the members of the community in their contest with their adversaries, and sometimes it refers to a way of life that becomes part of humankind's very being (1QS iv 23–24). Brown concludes, "If the Qumran sectarians were men who walked in the way of the Spirit of Truth, they were also men who had been cleansed by God's holy spirit which united them to God's truth (1QS iii 6–7)."[19] Without positing any direct link between the Johannine community and the Essenes of Qumran, it is interesting to note that both attribute the dual role of instruction and advocacy to this one they call the Spirit of truth.

In 16:8–11 (section a' of the chiasmus) the agenda of the Paraclete is described in more detail. That agenda addresses sin, righteousness, and judgment, and thus parallels the concerns of Jesus himself in 5:19–47. This agenda is now even more urgent because of "the world's" continued failure to recognize Jesus, despite his return to God (which for the Johannine community is a past event), and his concomitant overcoming of the world (16:33).[20] The testimony of the Paraclete is to "convict" (ἐλέγχω) the world in matters of sin, righteousness, and judgment. In other words, the world itself is to be persuaded of its errors (of which, presumably, the disciples are already convinced). The reasons for the conviction on the first two matters are presented adversatively (μέν . . . δέ). Thus, in the first case (16:9) the ὅτι identifies what the world has done wrong, while the second (v. 10) explains why the Paraclete has the task of convicting the world. The third point (v. 11) is simply appended with no particular link, but in that case too the explanation seems to provide the rationale for the Paraclete's action, namely that the world's judgment against Jesus has been proven wrong by the fact that Jesus has overcome the world (16:33).[21]

In verse 12 the focus shifts back to the disciples and their readiness to assume their own responsibility to testify. Within the story world—at the end of Jesus' life—the disciples have heard all they can "carry" (βαστάζω). The future task of guidance (literally, "leading them into the way [ὁδηγέω] into all the truth" [author's translation]) will belong to the Spirit of truth (v. 13), thus linking once again "way" and "truth" as in 14:6. In accomplishing these tasks the Spirit of truth once again fulfills the representative role, acting now on behalf of Jesus ("he will take what is mine and declare it to you"—v. 14) as well as of God ("all that the Father has is mine"—v. 15) to sustain their presence in this community.

CONCLUSION

For the Fourth Gospel, then, the Paraclete is related both to Christology and to ecclesiology. This ἄλλος παράκλητος continues into the time beyond Jesus' earthly life, God's ultimate engagement among humankind as Wisdom/σοφία, the λόγος become flesh. It is the form taken by divine Wisdom once again become flesh in the lives of the about-to-be-bereaved disciples, the Johannine community, and the church—communities of those befriended by Jesus and called to be friends of one another. These communities become the locus of Wisdom's persistent quest for a dwelling place in the homes and on the street corners where daily life is lived, and where she still meets rejection by the world that is hostile to her followers. Through the παράκλητος she continues to instruct her followers in what they need to know to understand the nature and ways of God, and to lead them into the "way" where they come to know the truth/the Spirit of truth itself, and in that knowing find the occasion of liberation (8:32).

Chapter 7

Conclusions and Implications

SUMMARY OF THIS STUDY

This study has demonstrated that one prominent thread in the intricate tapestry that expresses the Christology and ecclesiology of the Fourth Gospel is formed by the intertwining images of divine Wisdom and friendship. As Wisdom/ὁ λόγος, Jesus of Nazareth incarnates the creative will of God present from before time and seen in the creation in which that λόγος participated. Like Wisdom, Jesus/ὁ λόγος (now become flesh) unites God's work as creator with God's passion for a restored relationship with humankind. He embodies God's commitment to accompany God's people and to mediate to them life in its fullness, regardless of human failures. Just as Wisdom lives in the symbols of bread, water, and wine that bless and sustain physical life and point toward the essence of life not limited by human finitude, so Jesus is linked to these symbols in the narratives and discourses of the Fourth Gospel, and particularly in the "I AM" sayings. Jesus' obedience to God who "sent" him mirrors Wisdom's expression of God's identity as redeemer and sustainer as well as creator. Like Wisdom, whom only few discern and follow, Jesus also finds a mixed reception, and finally only a limited home among a small community of followers, who become the new community of "children" (John 1:12) or "friends" (15:12–17) of God. In that way, Wisdom, now become flesh in Jesus, functions not only as a christological category by which to identify Jesus, but also as an ecclesiological category that defines the center and the boundaries of the new community.

These images of Wisdom intertwine with images of friendship to amplify both the picture of Jesus' identity as the Christ and the character of the community formed in relationship to him. Jesus' "appointment" (the verb τίθημι) of his life on behalf of his friends is summarized in the vivid image of the model shepherd (John 10). The shepherd who shares daily life with the sheep, nurturing and caring for them, coming to know them by name, and becoming the "door" protecting them from harm lives the life of a friend among friends. That picture summarizes both the sayings about friendship in 15:12–17 and the Gospel narrative of the daily rhythms of Jesus' life with his friends and the examples of their solidarity in moments of crisis. His sharing of meals with his friends, tending them in times of illness, and teaching them the "way" and commandments that are his gift to them fulfills his vocation as Wisdom made flesh as well as his life of friendship. By so doing, Jesus fulfills the commission for which he has been sent, namely, to embody God's love for "the world" (3:16). He is the friend who befriends others and makes them into friends of one another in the community of his followers, both while he "encamps" with them (1:14) and after his "glorification" and resurrection. For the Fourth Gospel, then, an important hallmark of the church is both the gift and the demand of that friendship, so that the Gospel story and the life it conveys can continue beyond the time boundaries of the λόγος made flesh.

Crucial to the continuity between the story of Jesus and the life of the church according to the Fourth Gospel is the ἄλλος παράκλητος, who continues God's ultimate engagement among humankind as Wisdom/ὁ λόγος become flesh in the time after Jesus' earthly life. Because of the Paraclete, Wisdom once again becomes flesh in the lives of the about-to-be-bereaved disciples, the Johannine community, and the church. These communities become the new locus of Wisdom's persistent quest for a dwelling place where daily life is lived, where she instructs and leads followers in the "way" of God's truth, befriends them, and at the same time is rejected by a hostile world. As the παράκλητος Wisdom's liberating truth (John 8:32) is conveyed by one who is the Spirit of truth itself.

The images of friendship found in the Fourth Gospel reflect the Johannine community's roots in both the biblical traditions and the culture of the Hellenistic world. The images of Wisdom also resonate with that dual identity. They draw on the hope and promise carried in the Wisdom hymns that have spoken with special effectiveness to Jews who sought to live by their covenant with God in contexts of historical chaos and stress like that of the political and economic domination, cultural diversity, and religious pluralism of the Diaspora. That general context took on even sharper focus as the Johannine community faced a rupture in their relationship with the synagogue that had been their religious home. Whatever actually happened in that relationship, the Fourth Gospel reflects their experience as one of dislocation and disorientation. In that context, any word of good news in the Gospel would have to constellate a world that coheres even in the face of the chaos around them. Jesus as Wisdom/ὁ λόγος and as friend would also need to address basic human needs of safety and unshakeable companionship in the face of danger, the security of a "way" where there is no way, bread to satisfy deep hunger, and life itself—abundant life—that overcomes death.

PASTORAL AND THEOLOGICAL IMPLICATIONS

The picture of Jesus and the church defined by categories of divine Wisdom and friendship obviously does not exhaust the witness of the Fourth Gospel on the double-sided subject that encompasses Christology and ecclesiology. In fact, as I noted above, it is but one thread in a complex tapestry. Isolating that thread for closer examination has uncovered a number of subtle dimensions of the efforts of this writer to make the paradoxical affirmation that eventually found its way into the church's creeds, namely, that Jesus is at once fully human and fully divine. It has also demonstrated the interdependence of this picture of the Christ and the view of the community drawn together in Christ's name. Similarly, an examination of the thread that intertwines Wisdom and friendship as christological and ecclesiological categories has implications for the life of the contemporary church and its ministry. Like the images of Wisdom and friendship presented in the Fourth Gospel, those reflections also must be context specific. Therefore, instead of attempting to speak about "the church," or even about "the church" in my own context of North America or my own Reformed confessional tradition, I will offer reflections prompted by the intersection of my research on this project and my experiences as a participant-observer in Central America and with the Latino/Hispanic community in the United States. I will focus those reflections through the lens of a "ministry of accompaniment" as a rubric appropriate both to the unshakeable reliability of the friend who "appoints" his or her life for a friend, and to the persistent quest of Wisdom/ὁ λόγος for a home.

What one hears in the phrase "ministry of accompaniment" depends on whether one is speaking English or Spanish. In English the phrase a "ministry of accompaniment" sounds weak, like background music coincidental to the main activity or performance. Even with that meaning, however, the phrase bears revisiting, in order to allow us to think about ministry as something that, if it is done well, does not call attention to itself. Rather, it is barely noticed, so that what is perceived is others' work, and, more important, the gospel itself that is being "performed." In Spanish, however, the phrase itself is powerful. It evokes words like *compañero/a,* which designates someone with whom one shares *pan*—bread—and even life itself.

The verb *acompañar* is a term used in the various liberation movements of Central America, for example, to speak of or to address others in the movement with whom one is engaged in the struggle for life against the "idols of death," as the forces of the government, the military, and the dominant economic institutions, and their ruling ideologies are called. To speak of a ministry of accompaniment identifies one's ministry with that struggle as well. Such ministry entails entering into the life circumstances of one's community, giving up any position of privilege that might exempt one from the suffering experienced by the poorest of the people, who are often treated as nonpersons. They are especially vulnerable to hunger, disease, and the desperate poverty that pushes them to accept dangerous and underpaid employment in agriculture, manufacturing, and a variety of clandestine activities. These people are also particularly vulnerable to the officially sanctioned terrorism of police and military death squads. "Solidarity" is the word secular groups use for such absolutely unshakeable hanging-in together. The church calls it accompaniment. In Johannine language, it amounts to "appointing one's life for one's friends."

Sometimes in those contexts, and in far too many similar contexts around the world, "appointing one's life for one's friends" does entail martyrdom. But martyrdom is neither the point nor the purpose of *acompañamiento.* The purpose is engagement on behalf of life. The phrase *teología de la vida*—theology of life—affirms a commitment to the fundamental rights of each person to adequate food, clean water, shelter, medical care, and education, and to safety in one's dwelling and on the streets of one's neighborhood. The goal of the quest is life in all its fullness. When death comes in the course of that struggle, it is because the message of life is intolerable to those who view life as a privilege of the rich and powerful, and who bend their tremendous power to limiting access to it. But the struggle for life is a joyful one, and it is a celebration of community, of "a people defined by relationship, with each other, the world, and God."[1] In form it entails a living out of the model of friendship encountered in John's Gospel. In content it reflects the identity of Jesus as divine Wisdom/ὁ λόγος, the friend who makes others into friends of God, neighbor, and self.

Several implications follow from these observations. First, attention to the Fourth Gospel and its call to form a community of Wisdom's friends draws us toward our most vulnerable neighbors as those around whom and with whom the community takes shape. Persons who are most vulnerable to physical threats of hunger, homelessness, illness, and random and focused violence, and to threats of isolation from family members, from many religious institutions and communities as well as from institutions and communities of the secular society, and from the material and psychological benefits of the common life are those whom the Fourth Gospel calls us to accompany—to stand beside them when others flee and to refuse to be moved.

Accompanying them—befriending these neighbors in the Johannine sense— requires first that we get to know them and allow our worlds to be transformed by their worlds and their stories. As a result, each act we perform and each step we take is done with full cognizance of its effect for good or ill on the neighbors whose fate has become our own. A piece of that task involves wisdom in the sense of knowledge, making the effort to become informed about others' realities and how they are shaped, instead of resting with the relative comfort of ignorance about the ways our apparently innocent choices can spell death for others. This wisdom entails information and intellectual understanding of the ways our world functions, including even such obscure and complex sectors as international economics and the politics of health care delivery.

Just as important, however, is the wisdom that is heart-wisdom—compassion and the ability to know in the depths of our being the reality of which another speaks, to feel with others at that core of our being that galvanizes us into action. Feeling in this "wise" sense is not a purely emotional response, in distinction from knowing, but rather it picks up on the meaning of the Spanish verb *sentir*. As Roberto Goizueta observes,

> In Spanish . . . the verb *sentir* connotes, not feelings *per se,* but an experiential form of knowledge, or perception, involving the whole person: "It does not concern a sentimental 'feeling' ['*sentir*'], but one which is sapiential and ethical, that is, of the 'heart.' " To *sentir* with the poor person is to be one with her or him affectively and ethico-politically, and, thus, to know her or him. To *sentir* God's presence is to be *affectively* united to God, to *do* God's will, and thus to *know* God.[2]

It is, in other words, a wisdom that dares the love, intimacy, and friendship that can only emerge when people accompany one another through the rhythms of daily life and hang in together, come what may.

A ministry of accompaniment includes not allowing ourselves the protection of privilege, taking refuge behind the layers of insolation our positions, our class, our race provide for us. A ministry of accompaniment might entail direct political action together with those being excluded from basic human social rights of *pan y techo*—food and shelter—in our cities and rural areas, or those whom the schools are not teaching and whose health care is left to the triage practiced in emergency rooms when their situation becomes desperate. Such a ministry also might entail daring to use whatever public voices we have as pastors, teachers, or other community leaders to remind people that, regardless of the private ledgers of personal morality any of us manage to complete for ourselves, we and the society that sustains us and from which we benefit will be judged by how we treat our most vulnerable neighbors. Those neighbors are any whom the decisions of our lives touch, be they members of our own families or of our communities, other citizens and documented or undocumented residents of our land, or people whose lives are shaped by the global economy that has one of its key bases in the United States.

I would suggest that the Fourth Gospel, which has so long been dismissed—or lauded—as the "spiritual" or "otherworldly" Gospel, is among our richest resources for this pastoral and educational task. As it chronicles the embrace of Christ by the community of Wisdom's friends, this Gospel pushes its readers to recognize the very earthly, political implications of the heavenly Wisdom disclosed to us by the only one who has seen God and who reveals God's Wisdom to those who receive her in him. This Gospel also makes clear that what is required by the commandment to love one another, God also makes possible by the initiating love of Christ for his "friends." Those who are Jesus' "friends" and who love one another are accompanied in utter constancy by God in Jesus Christ. These friends are then able to accompany others because the Advocate dwells in and among them. They have been born "again" or "from above," into a new reality, which for the author of the Fourth Gospel clearly means a new community. They get by with more than a little help from their friends, because they are not left alone or comfortless. Instead Wisdom dwells among them, full of grace and truth, a light shining in deepest night, a Word of life.

Notes

PREFACE

1. Hans Dieter Betz, *Galatians* (Hermeneia; Philadelphia: Fortress Press, 1979), 220–37.
2. The Re-imagining Conference, "Re-imagining . . . God, Community, the Church," was held in Minneapolis, Minnesota, November 4–7, 1993, under the sponsorship of the Churches in Solidarity Committee of the Greater Minneapolis/St. Paul Area and the Minnesota Council of Churches. The Ecumenical Decade was a program emphasis of the World Council of Churches.
3. Neither the translations of biblical texts nor the scholarly discussions of them are consistent on the question of whether to capitalize the word "wisdom." In this study I have followed the sources when I have quoted them. In my own work, I have capitalized the word when it refers to the embodied figure ("Ms. Wisdom," as it were), and left it in lowercase when it refers to a quality of knowledge or a category of thought or of literature. Unfortunately, the line between these uses is often unclear, both in the biblical texts and in scholarly debates about them.

CHAPTER 1: WISDOM AND FRIENDSHIP: IMAGES OF CHRIST AND CHURCH

1. Diego Irarrázaval, "La otra globalización—anotación teológica," *Pasos* 77 (1998): 2.
2. "I Am For You"; © 1987 The Iona Community; in *Heaven Shall Not Wait* (rev. ed.; John Bell and Graham Maule, eds.; Chicago: Wild Goose Publications, GIA Publications, Inc., 1989), 11 (used with permission).
3. Studies that affirm the presence of a "Wisdom Christology" in the Fourth Gospel have flourished in the final decade of the twentieth century. Some of the most significant ones are: Michael E. Willett, *Wisdom Christology in the Fourth Gospel* (San Francisco: Mellen Research University Press, 1992); Martin Scott, *Sophia and the Johannine Jesus* (JSNTSup 71; Sheffield: Sheffield Academic Press, 1992); Ben Witherington, III, *John's Wisdom: A Commentary on the Fourth Gospel* (Louisville, Ky.: Westminster John Knox Press, 1995); Elisabeth Schüssler Fiorenza, *Jesus: Miriam's Child, Sophia's Prophet: Critical Issues in Feminist Christology* (New York: Continuum, 1994), 152–54; Elizabeth A. Johnson, *She Who Is: The Mystery of God in Feminist Theological Discourse* (New York: Crossroad, 1994), 96–99.
4. Willett, *Wisdom Christology,* 26.
5. Dwight N. Hopkins notes that among African American slaves in the United States, friendship was a crucial and valued relationship, and that role was attributed to Jesus as well. "Slaves deeply cherished friendship," he observes; "under their circumstances, a friend was one with whom you literally trusted your life. . . . For the slaves, Jesus the 'bosom friend' ceaselessly and consistently destroyed the 'blocks' of the devilish slave system and thereby thwarted death and preserved black life" (*Shoes That Fit Our Feet: Sources for a Constructive Black Theology* [Maryknoll, N.Y.: Orbis Books, 1994], 31–32).
6. Mary E. Hunt, *Fierce Tenderness: A Feminist Theology of Friendship* (New York: Crossroad, 1991).

7. Sallie McFague, *Models of God: Theology for an Ecological, Nuclear Age* (Philadelphia: Fortress Press, 1987), 157–80.

8. Josephine Massyngbaerde Ford, *Redeemer, Friend, and Mother: Salvation in Antiquity and in the Gospel of John* (Minneapolis: Fortress Press, 1997); Eldo Puthenkandathil, *Philos: A Designation for the Jesus-Disciple Relationship: An Exegetico-Theological Investigation of the Term in the Fourth Gospel* (Frankfurt: Peter Lang, 1993).

9. Jürgen Roloff, *Die Kirche im Neuen Testament* (Grundrisse zum Neuen Testament 10; Göttingen: Vandenhoeck & Ruprecht, 1993), 299–300.

10. Jürgen Moltmann, *The Passion for Life: A Messianic Lifestyle* (Philadelphia: Fortress Press, 1977), 57–62.

11. Elizabeth Johnson (*She Who Is,* 165) summarizes this link between the identity of Jesus as Wisdom (Sophia) and the identity of the church as follows: "Sophia's intimate solidarity with the unoriginate God and her equally compassionate, life-giving solidarity with human beings whom she makes into friends of God are embodied in Jesus-Sophia, whose person is constituted by these two fundamental relations."

12. Paul S. Minear, "Logos Ecclesiology in John's Gospel," in *Christological Perspectives: Essays in Honor of Harvey K. McArthur* (ed. Robert F. Berkey and Sarah A. Edwards; New York: Pilgrim Press, 1982), 95–111.

13. Ibid., 106.

14. Ibid., 108.

15. Johan Ferreira, *Johannine Ecclesiology* (JSNTSup 160; Sheffield: Sheffield Academic Press, 1998), 35–44. See also the discussion in Raymond E. Brown, *The Gospel according to John* (AB 29; Garden City, N.Y.: Doubleday & Co., 1966), cv–cxi.

16. Ernst Käsemann, *The Testament of Jesus: A Study of the Fourth Gospel in the Light of Chapter 17* (Philadelphia: Fortress Press, 1968). Käsemann emphasizes, however, that the Fourth Gospel has no explicit ecclesiology in the sense of a structural concept of the church (p. 27).

17. Rudolf Schnackenburg, *The Gospel according to St. John* (3 vols.; New York: Crossroad, 1987), 1:154–64.

18. Wes Howard-Brook, *Becoming Children of God: John's Gospel and Radical Discipleship* (Maryknoll, N.Y.: Orbis Books, 1994), 33.

19. Ibid., 212.

20. Because it is impossible to separate Christology and ecclesiology, the conclusion of Witherington that the focus in the Fourth Gospel is on Christology and "only secondarily and in a few places (e.g., John 13–17; John 21) on matters of discipleship and community life" (Witherington, *John's Wisdom,* 1) cannot be true. To say further that the Fourth Gospel appears to have been written for missionary and evangelistic work, and not for or about the church (*ibid.,* 2), seems to draw a false and unnecessary contrast. I would argue instead that, precisely because of the centrality of Christology in the Fourth Gospel, the meaning and identity of the church are at its heart.

21. Sallie McFague, *Metaphorical Theology: Models of God in Religious Language* (Philadelphia: Fortress Press, 1982).

22. Schüssler Fiorenza, *Jesus,* 161.

23. For a discussion of my understanding of the role of images in christological reflection, see Sharon H. Ringe, *Jesus, Liberation, and the Biblical Jubilee: Images for Ethics and Christology* (OBT; Philadelphia: Fortress Press, 1985), 6–13.

24. Robert Gordon Maccini, *Her Testimony Is True: Women as Witnesses according to John* (JSNTSup 125; Sheffield: Sheffield Academic Press, 1996).

CHAPTER 2: GETTING TO KNOW THE JOHANNINE COMMUNITY

1. Ben Witherington, III (*John's Wisdom: A Commentary on the Fourth Gospel* [Louisville, Ky.: Westminster John Knox Press, 1995], 1), emphasizes that any reflection on the life of the community is secondary to the author's christological purpose. On one level that

is true, since the overt subject is Jesus, but the account of Jesus' life and teaching is pastoral, and thus it is tied closely to the needs and beliefs of that community, at least as the author perceives them.

2. Although W. D. Davies ("Reflections on Aspects of the Jewish Background of the Gospel of John," in *Exploring the Gospel of John: In Honor of D. Moody Smith* [ed. R. Alan Culpepper and C. Clifton Black; Louisville, Ky.: Westminster John Knox Press, 1996], 43–64), is careful to demonstrate the complex relationships between various Jewish communities and the institutions and cultures that surround them, he nevertheless posits a reconstruction of "Jamnia" as the center of a consolidated and increasingly homogeneous Judaism after 70 C.E. That conclusion is certainly justified over the long term, but it seems to me to introduce an anachronistic note for the late first century, when this Gospel was written.

3. For discussions of the specific date of this Gospel, see the introductions to such commentaries as Rudolf Schnackenburg, *The Gospel according to St. John* (3 vols.; New York: Crossroad, 1987), 1:59–104; Raymond E. Brown, *The Gospel according to John* (AB 29; Garden City, N.Y.: Doubleday & Co., 1966); Wes Howard-Brook, *Becoming Children of God: John's Gospel and Radical Discipleship* (Maryknoll, N.Y.: Orbis Books, 1994); or Witherington, *John's Wisdom.*

4. See the discussion in Robert T. Fortna, *The Fourth Gospel and Its Predecessors* (Philadelphia: Fortress Press, 1988), which is a revision of the argument of his earlier work, *The Gospel of Signs: A Reconstruction of the Narrative Source Underlying the Fourth Gospel* (SNTSMS 11; Cambridge: Cambridge University Press, 1970).

5. W. D. Davies, "Reflections on Aspects of the Jewish Background of the Gospel of John," 44; Gerard Sloyan, *John* (Interpretation; Atlanta: John Knox Press, 1988), 3, 7. For a discussion of the phenomenon I have called "immigrant language," see Ngugi wa Thiong'o, "The Language of African Literature," in *The Post-Colonial Studies Reader* (ed. Bill Ashcroft, Gareth Griffiths, and Helen Tiffin; London and New York: Routledge, 1995), 285–90.

6. Witherington, *John's Wisdom,* 13.

7. This hypothesis is presented and defended in Obery M. Hendricks, "A Discourse of Domination: A Socio-Rhetorical Study of the Use of *Ioudaios* in the Fourth Gospel" (Ph.D. diss., Princeton University, 1995).

8. James H. Charlesworth, "The Dead Sea Scrolls and the Gospel according to John," in *Exploring the Gospel of John,* 65–97; Brown, *John,* 1:lxii–lxiii; Schnackenburg, *St. John,* 1.135; Howard-Brook, 30–31.

9. Brown, *John,* AB 29A, lxxiii.

10. Brown, *John,* AB 29A, lxxiii, cliii–civ; Gale A. Yee, *Jewish Feasts and the Gospel of John* (Wilmington, Del.: Michael Glazier, 1989), 12; Schnackenburg, *St. John,* 1:152; Adele Reinhartz, "The Gospel of John," in *Searching the Scriptures: Volume Two: A Feminist Commentary* (ed. Elisabeth Schüssler Fiorenza; New York: Crossroad, 1994), 562.

11. Reinhartz, "John," 562.

12. Witherington, *John's Wisdom,* 19.

13. Brown, *John,* AB 29A, lix–lx.

14. This conclusion is shared by most contemporary Johannine scholars. See, for example, Sloyan, *John,* 3, 7; Howard-Brook, *Becoming Children of God,* 30–31; Davies, "Reflections," 43; Charlesworth, "The Dead Sea Scrolls and the Gospel according to John," 66; Schnackenburg, *St. John,* 1:119–21; Yee, *Jewish Feasts,* 16, 20; Brown, *John,* AB 29A, lvi; Witherington, *John's Wisdom,* 12; R. Alan Culpepper, *Anatomy of the Fourth Gospel: A Study in Literary Design* (Philadelphia: Fortress Press, 1983), 211–23; Raymond E. Brown, *The Community of the Beloved Disciple: The Life, Loves, and Hates of an Individual Church in New Testament Times* (New York: Paulist Press, 1979), 22, 26–36.

15. Brown, *Community,* 34–40.

16. Brown, *Community,* 55–58; Kiyoshi Tsuchido, " "Ελλην in the Gospel of John: Tradition and Redaction in John 12:20–24," in *The Conversation Continues: Studies in Paul and John in Honor of J. Louis Martyn* (ed. Robert T. Fortna and Beverly R. Gaventa; Nashville: Abingdon Press, 1990), 348–50. Martin Scott (*Sophia and the Johannine Jesus* [JSNTSup 71; Sheffield: Sheffield Academic Press, 1992], 35) assumes the presence of Gentiles and Samaritans in the Johannine community on the basis of the mention of those groups in the Gospel, but he does not argue the case.

17. Peder Borgen, "The Gospel of John and Hellenism: Some Observations," in *Exploring the Gospel of John,* 98–123.

18. J. Louis Martyn, "A Gentile Mission That Replaced an Earlier Jewish Mission?," in *Exploring the Gospel of John,* 124–44. Note that, on the contrary, Witherington (*John's Wisdom,* 33) asserts that a Gentile mission did characterize the Johannine community.

19. Yee, *Jewish Feasts,* 26–30.

20. See the discussion in Scott (*Sophia,* 174–240). I am indebted also to a seminar paper presented by Rebecca E. Duke at Wesley Theological Seminary, which analyzed the function of the women characters in advancing the narrative development of the Fourth Gospel.

21. Michael E. Willett, *Wisdom Christology in the Fourth Gospel* (San Francisco: Mellen Research University Press, 1992), 146.

22. Howard-Brook, *Becoming Children of God,* 32.

23. See discussions of the identity of the "beloved disciple" in Brown, *Community,* 34; Witherington, *John's Wisdom,* 14; Schnackenburg, *St. John,* 3:375–88.

24. Bernadette J. Brooten, *Women Leaders in the Ancient Synagogue* (BJS 36; Chico, Calif.: Scholars Press, 1982).

25. Howard-Brook, *Becoming Children of God,* 49.

26. This is the subject developed in Robert J. Karris, *Jesus and the Marginalized in John's Gospel* (Wilmington, Del.: Michael Glazier, 1990).

27. Howard-Brook, *Becoming Children of God,* 47; Brown, *John* (AB 19), lix; Schnackenburg, *St. John,* 1:124.

28. For this reason I cannot accept the conclusion of Tina Pippin (" 'For Fear of the Jews': Lying and Truth-Telling in Translating the Gospel of John," *Semeia* 76 [1996]: 82) that the term refers to "a monolithic group of 'enemies,' " and that all efforts to see it as more nuanced are simply efforts to rescue the text from its fundamentally "anti-Jewish" position (88).

29. See the discussions of this controversial term in Schnackenburg, *St. John,* 1:165; Yee, *Jewish Feasts,* 14–15; Howard-Brook, *Becoming Children of God,* 41; Brown, *John,* lxvii–lxxiii; Wayne A. Meeks, " 'Am I a Jew?'—Johannine Christianity and Judaism," in *Christianity, Judaism and Other Greco-Roman Cults—Part One: New Testament* (4 vols.; SJLA 12; ed. Jacob Neusner; Leiden: E. J. Brill, 1975), 1:163–86.

30. Witherington (*John's Wisdom,* 12) suggests that this Gospel thus has in view an opposition to Jesus from Jewish religious leaders that long predates the context of the Johannine community.

31. Again, the dissertation of Obery M. Hendricks ("A Discourse of Domination") provides supporting evidence for that conclusion.

32. Urban C. von Wahlde, "The Terms for Religious Authorities in the Fourth Gospel: A Key to Literary Strata?" *JBL* 98 (1979): 231–53; John Ashton, "The Identity and Function of the *Ioudaioi* in the Fourth Gospel," *NovT* 27 (1985): 40–75.

33. Yee (*Jewish Feasts,* 15) makes a similar point.

34. J. Louis Martyn, *History and Theology in the Fourth Gospel,* rev. ed. (Nashville: Abingdon Press, 1979). Martyn's hypothesis has been followed, with some variations in details by (among others) Davies, "Reflections," 47–56; Charlesworth, "The Dead Sea Scrolls and the Gospel according to John," 75; Howard-Brook, *Becoming Children of God,* 20; Tsuchido, " "Ελλην in the Gospel of John," 349; Schnackenburg, *St.*

John, 1:166; Brown, *John,* AB 29A, lxxxiv; Brown, *Community,* 17, 22, 40–43; M. C. DeBoer, *Johannine Perspectives on the Death of Jesus* (Kampen: Kok Pharos, 1996), 53–70; David Rensberger, *Johannine Faith and Liberating Community* (Philadelphia: Westminster Press, 1988), 25–26. Two scholars whose published work diverges most sharply from the near consensus are Yee (*Jewish Feasts,* 22–24) and Witherington (*John's Wisdom,* 7).

35. As Howard-Brook points out (*Becoming Children of God,* 28), it is unclear whether the community's defense of Jesus as messiah by appealing to specific texts of Hebrew scriptures would even have been a comprehensible strategy to most Jews, at least of this period. Such a confession would have fallen so far outside of their religious thought world that it would hardly have been identified as a threat to anyone's authority.

36. See the discussion in Howard Brook, *Becoming Children of God,* 28–29, and Urban C. von Wahlde, "Community in Conflict: The History and Social Context of the Johannine Community," *Int* 49 (1995): 382–84.

37. "The early Christian mutation" is the way Larry Hurtado characterizes this striking discontinuity that disrupts an underlying continuity with ancient Jewish monotheism. See Larry W. Hurtado, *One God, One Lord: Early Christian Devotion and Ancient Jewish Monotheism* (Philadelphia: Fortress Press, 1988), 93–124.

38. The following proposal was prompted by a conversation with Adele Reinhartz, who has not published this specific suggestion as an alternative to the Martyn hypothesis. Her article, "The Johannine Community and Its Jewish Neighbors: A Reappraisal" (in *"What Is John?",* vol. 2: *Literary and Social Readings of the Fourth Gospel* [SBL Symposium Series 7; ed. Fernando F. Segovia; Atlanta: Scholars Press, 1998], 111–38) argues against the proposal fundamental to the Martyn hypothesis, namely, that the Gospel presents a two-level drama that relates simultaneously the life of Jesus and the experiences of the Johannine community. Her conclusion to that article moves in a direction close to that reflected here: "By explaining the Gospel's problematic portrayal of Jews as a consequence of the community's ongoing struggle for self-definition rather than as an external, Jewish act of expulsion removes responsibility for the anti-Jewish language from late first-century Jews or their authorities and restores it to the Johannine community, which embedded this portrayal in its formative text" (138).

39. Bruce J. Malina (*The Social World of Jesus and the Gospel* [London and New York: Routledge, 1996], 222–36) examines a later period in the life of this same community, when it is considering the implications of welcoming outsiders into an already formed community. He speaks of this process in terms of the transformation of the outsider's status from stranger to guest. The process I see as having happened in the community from which the Fourth Gospel emerged describes the reverse movement relative to the members' status in the synagogue community—the transformation from full members, to conditional participants (as their beliefs in Jesus became firmer and more fully articulated), to strangers no longer at home there. At the same time, the Johannine Christians would have been refining practices and rules of hospitality to manage the boundaries of their own community.

40. In the case of the Johannine community, for example, the issue raised is not to identify the legitimate heirs of Abraham, but rather to make the case for the necessity of "rebirth" (1:11–13; 3:3–8; 9:2–7) and the presence of the spirit of God (14:16, 26; 15:26; 16:7). See Howard-Brook, *Becoming Children of God,* 29.

41. See Adele Reinhartz, "From Narrative to History: The Resurrection of Mary and Martha," in *"Women like This": New Perspectives on Jewish Women in the Greco-Roman World* (Early Judaism and Its Literature 1; ed. Amy-Jill Levine; Atlanta: Scholars Press, 1991), 160–84.

42. J. Louis Martyn develops this argument in *The Gospel of John in Christian History* (New York: Paulist Press, 1978).

43. As Howard-Brook observes (*Becoming Children of God,* 17), the Fourth Gospel is "a

conscious *selection* of *historical* stories, told with the particular *ideological* goal of leading readers to faith in Jesus, through a complex and absorbing *aesthetic* structure and style." In this summary, he echoes the position of Meir Sternberg, *The Poetics of Biblical Narrative* (Bloomington: Indiana University Press, 1985), 44. Witherington (*John's Wisdom,* 3–4) joins R. Burridge (*What Are the Gospels?* [Cambridge: Cambridge University Press, 1991]) in identifying the canonical Gospels in general, and the Gospel of John in particular, as representatives of the genre of ancient biography. Criteria that place it in this genre are the presence of a prologue or introduction; the focus on a particular individual; organization of the material according to topical, chronological, and geographical categories; the focus on deeds and teachings that reveal the individual's character, particularly those that present it in a positive light and that are designed to evoke the reader's reverence; and a length that is longer than a speech, but one which would still fit on a single scroll.

44. They are so identified only in 6:67, 70, 71; and 20:24.
45. Schnackenburg, *St. John,* 1:42.
46. See the discussion of the relationship between the Johannine community and other early Christian communities connected to the Synoptic Gospels in Howard-Brook, *Becoming Children of God,* 20–21, 34–35, 45; Rensberger, *Johannine Faith,* 27; Witherington, *John's Wisdom,* 5–9; Brown, *Community,* 81–91; Brown, *John,* xliv–xlvii; Schnackenburg, *St. John,* 1:26–43; Jerome H. Neyrey, *An Ideology of Revolt: John's Christology in Social-Science Perspective* (Philadelphia: Fortress Press, 1988), 6.
47. See the discussions of the date of the Fourth Gospel in Witherington, *John's Wisdom,* 28–29; Scott, *Sophia,* 35; Howard-Brook, *Becoming Children of God,* 20; Yee, *Jewish Feasts,* 12; Brown, *John,* AB 29A, lxxx–lxxxvi; von Wahlde, "Terms for Religious Authorities," 379–82.
48. On the process of composition of the Fourth Gospel, see Sloyan, *John,* 3; Scott, *Sophia,* 35; Yee, *Jewish Feasts,* 12–13; Witherington, *John's Wisdom,* 9–11, 19; Charlesworth, "The Dead Sea Scrolls and the Gospel according to John," 79; Schnackenburg, *St. John,* 1:153; 3.381; von Wahlde, "Terms for Religious Authorities," 379–89; Brown, *Community,* 22–23, 25–91; Brown, *John,* AB 29A, xxxlv.
49. Sloyan, *John,* 3; Brown, *John,* AB 29A, xxiv–xxxix.
50. In this conclusion, I disagree with Witherington (*John's Wisdom,* 2, 39–40), who identifies mission and evangelism as important agenda of the Johannine community.
51. Wayne A. Meeks, "The Man from Heaven in Johannine Sectarianism," *JBL* 91 (1972): 44–72.

CHAPTER 3: THE ROOTS OF WISDOM

1. Roland E. Murphy, "Wisdom—Theses and Hypotheses," in *Israelite Wisdom: Theological and Literary Essays in Honor of Samuel Terrien* (ed. John G. Gammie et al.; Missoula, Mont.: Scholars Press, 1978), 37; Leo G. Perdue, *Wisdom and Creation: The Theology of Wisdom Literature* (Nashville: Abingdon Press, 1994), 52.
2. See the discussion in Michael E. Willett, *Wisdom Christology in the Fourth Gospel* (San Francisco: Mellen Research University Press, 1992), 26–31.
3. Willett (*Wisdom Christology,* 23–26) summarizes the current state of the discussion of whether to conceptualize Wisdom-in-human-form as hypostasis, personification, myth, metaphor, or symbol. The search for both the term's precision and its elasticity at the same time is related to the appropriateness of Wisdom categories in the christological reflection of the early church, as discussed in chap. 1.
4. For a discussion of the social construction of the feminine in the wisdom literature, see Carole R. Fontaine, "The Social Roles of Women in the World of Wisdom," in *A Feminist Companion to Wisdom Literature* (ed. Athalya Brenner; Sheffield: Sheffield Academic Press, 1995), 27–49. Claudia V. Camp identifies the ambivalent power that the figures of Wisdom and her negative parallel, the "foreign" or "strange" woman, have

for women, as follows: "As female images constructed by men, they are in one sense inherently disempowering for women; they inhibit our ability to name and shape ourselves by telling us in advance who we are and may become. On the other hand, as *powerful* female images they tantalize the female questor/questioner of power." ("The Woman Wisdom and the Strange Woman: Where Is Power to be Found?," in *Reading Bibles, Writing Bodies: Identity and the Book* [ed. Timothy K. Beal and David M. Gunn; London and New York: Routledge, 1996], 85.)

5. The development of Sophia traditions in the literature of Gnostic communities reflects a development subsequent to the Fourth Gospel. A discussion of that development can be found in Deirdre J. Good, *Reconstructing the Tradition of Sophia in Gnostic Literature* (SBLMS 32; Atlanta: Scholars Press, 1987).

6. Walter Brueggemann, *Israel's Praise: Doxology against Idolatry and Ideology* (Philadelphia: Fortress Press, 1988), 101; Patrick D. Miller, Jr., *Interpreting the Psalms* (Philadelphia: Fortress Press, 1986), 71.

7. Walter Brueggemann, *The Message of the Psalms: A Theological Commentary* (Minneapolis: Augsburg Publishing House, 1984), 32.

8. Leo G. Perdue, *Wisdom in Revolt: Metaphorical Theology in the Book of Job* (JSOTSup 112; Bible and Literature Series 29; Sheffield: JSOT Press [Almond Press], 1991), 242–44.

9. I agree with Carol A. Newsom (*The Book of Job* [NIB; Nashville: Abingdon Press, 1996] 4:531–33) against Leo G. Perdue (*Wisdom in Revolt*, 245) and Norman C. Habel (*The Book of Job: A Commentary* [OTL; Philadelphia: Westminster Press, 1985], 398–401) that there is no suggestion in this hymn of wisdom as an active presence or even a goddess who deliberately hides herself so that human beings cannot know her. In Job, God is the controlling agent, and one's relationship to God determines whether one will find wisdom.

10. That Job does make such a discovery is precisely Habel's affirmation (Habel, *Job*, 393). See also Gustavo Gutiérrez, *On Job: God-talk and the Suffering of the Innocent* (Maryknoll, N.Y.: Orbis Books, 1987), 38, 116 n. 9; and Carol A. Newsom, "Job," in *The Women's Bible Commentary* (ed. Carol A. Newsom and Sharon H. Ringe; Louisville, Ky.: Westminster John Knox, expanded edition, 1998), 142–43.

11. Michael V. Fox ("Ideas of Wisdom in Proverbs 1–9," *JBL* 116 [1987]: 613–33) argues, however, that another view of women exists alongside of this one. The other one, which may reflect a distinct source or voice in the book, views women, and Wisdom herself, as objects of aesthetic appreciation—passive, with no concrete accomplishments to their credit.

12. Athalya Brenner, "Proverbs 1–9: An F Voice?," in Brenner and Fokkelien Van Dijk-Hemmes, *On Gendering Texts: Female and Male Voices in the Hebrew Bible* (Leiden and New York: E. J. Brill, 1993), 113–30; Carol A. Newsom, "Woman and the Discourse of Patriarchal Wisdom: A Study of Proverbs 1–9," in *Gender and Difference in Ancient Israel* (ed. Peggy L. Day; Minneapolis: Fortress Press, 1989), 142–60.

13. Newsom, "Woman and the Discourse of Patriarchal Wisdom," 145–46.

14. Ibid., 149.

15. Ibid., 157.

16. Brenner, "Proverbs," 126; see also Claudia V. Camp, *Wisdom and the Feminine in the Book of Proverbs* (Bible and Literature Series 11; Sheffield: JSOT Press [Almond Press], 1985), 274.

17. Claudia V. Camp, "What's So Strange about the Strange Woman?," in *The Bible and the Politics of Exegesis: Essays in Honor of Norman K. Gottwald on His Sixty-Fifth Birthday* (ed. David Jobling et al.; Cleveland: Pilgrim Press, 1991).

18. Perdue, *Wisdom and Creation*, 93.

19. Bruce Vawter, "Prov. 8:22: Wisdom and Creation," *JBL* 99 (1980): 205–16.

20. See Judith E. McKinley, *Gendering Wisdom the Host: Biblical Invitations to Eat and Drink* (*JSOT* 216; Gender, Culture, Theory 4; Sheffield: Sheffield Academic Press,

1996) for a discussion of this dimension of Wisdom's role. Her study encompasses all instances in the Bible where food and drink are offered or provided.

21. Martin Scott, *Sophia and the Johannine Jesus* (JSNTSup 71; Sheffield: Sheffield Academic Press, 1992), 53.

22. Camp, *Wisdom and the Feminine*, 272.

23. J. N. Aletti, "Séduction et Parole en Proverbes I–IX," *VT* 27 (1977): 143.

24. This book is also known by the titles Ben Sira and Ecclesiasticus.

25. Fragments of manuscripts in Hebrew have been found at Qumran and Masada, though the only complete text in existence is in Greek. George W. E. Nickelsburg, *Jewish Literature between the Bible and the Mishnah: A Historical and Literary Introduction* (Philadelphia: Fortress Press, 1981), 64–65; Scott, *Sophia*, 53–54 n. 3.

26. James L. Crenshaw, *Old Testament Wisdom: An Introduction* (Atlanta: John Knox Press, 1981), 149.

27. Ibid., 152.

28. This is the suggestion of Perdue, *Wisdom and Creation*, 264; Nickelsburg, *Jewish Literature*, 60; R. A. F. MacKenzie, *Sirach* (OT Message 19; Wilmington, Del.: Michael Glazier, 1983), 101; and John G. Snaith, *Ecclesiasticus or The Wisdom of Jesus Son of Sirach* (New York and Cambridge: Cambridge University Press, 1974), 4. It is an issue implicit in the discussions of the apparent connection in content, if not in literary dependence, between the hymns to personified Wisdom and those to Isis. See the discussions in Burton L. Mack, *Logos und Sophia: Untersuchungen zur Weisheitstheologie im hellenistischen Judentum* (Göttingen: Vandenhoeck & Ruprecht, 1973), 38–42; Elisabeth Schüssler Fiorenza, *Jesus: Miriam's Child, Sophia's Prophet: Critical Issues in Feminist Christology* (New York: Continuum, 1994), 136–37; and Jack T. Sanders, *Ben Sira and Demotic Wisdom* (SBLMS 28; Chico, Calif.: Scholars Press, 1983), 45–50.

29. Nickelsburg, *Jewish Literature*, 60.

30. Mack, *Wisdom and the Hebrew Epic*, 152–53; Scott, *Sophia*, 55.

31. Crenshaw, *Old Testament Wisdom*, 187; David G. Burke, *The Poetry of Baruch: A Reconstruction and Analysis of the Original Hebrew Text of Baruch 3:9–5:9* (Chico, Calif.: Scholars Press, 1982), 26–32; Walter Harrelson, "Wisdom Hidden and Revealed according to Baruch (Baruch 3.9–4.4)," in *Priests, Prophets and Scribes: Essays on the Formation and Heritage of Second Temple Judaism in Honour of Joseph Blenkinsopp* (JSOTSup 149; ed. Eugene Ulrich et al.; Sheffield: Sheffield Academic Press, 1992), 159.

32. Nickelsburg, *Jewish Literature*, 112.

33. Although the book clearly dates from a period much later than that of King Solomon and probably owes nothing to him beyond his reputation, I have chosen that designation (and its abbreviation Wisd. Sol.) instead of the shorter title, "Wisdom," in order to be clear that the book is intended, and not the principle, quality, or personified figure.

34. Silvia Schroer, "The Book of Sophia," in *Searching the Scriptures*, vol. 2: *A Feminist Commentary* (ed. Elisabeth Schüssler Fiorenza; New York: Crossroad, 1994), 17–38. While Schroer treats Wisd. Sol. 6:1–11 as Wisdom's own introduction to the portrait that follows (23), Nickelsburg (*Jewish Literature*, 175) treats it as the conclusion of the first section. A case could be made for either reading.

35. Schroer, "Book of Sophia," 22–23.

36. Nickelsburg, *Jewish Literature*, 181; see also Perdue's discussion of παιδεία as discipline shaped by the desire for wisdom, piety, study, and obedience that assures immortality and the gift of sovereignty (*Wisdom and Creation*, 303).

37. Perdue, *Wisdom and Creation*, 309; Nickelsburg, *Jewish Literature*, 181; Scott, *Sophia*, 55–56.

38. Crenshaw, *Old Testament Wisdom*, 176.

39. Schroer, "Book of Sophia," 23.

40. Ibid., 33.

41. Nickelsburg, *Jewish Literature,* 180.
42. Schüssler Fiorenza, *Jesus: Miriam's Child, Sophia's Prophet,* 136.
43. Perdue, *Wisdom and Creation,* 304.
44. Schroer, "Book of Sophia," 34.
45. For a summary of Philo's writings on Wisdom, see Willett, *Wisdom Christology,* 18–20.
46. See Philo's portrait of this community and their male counterparts in his *De Vita Contemplativa,* and the discussion of the community in Ross Shepard Kraemer, *Her Share of the Blessings: Women's Religions among Pagans, Jews, and Christians in the Greco-Roman World* (New York: Oxford University Press, 1992), 113–17.
47. To call Philo a bridge figure, however, leaves an important question unanswered: Did the author of the Fourth Gospel actually know the works of Philo, or did they only share a common background in the popular culture of their day? In either case, their common use of λόγος as a kind of substitute for Wisdom supports the suggestion that the Fourth Gospel, like Philo, may have come from Alexandria.

CHAPTER 4: WISDOM MADE FLESH

1. See the discussions of these issues in such sources as Martin Scott (*Sophia and the Johannine Jesus* [JSNTSup 71; Sheffield: Sheffield Academic Press, 1992]; Alison Jasper, *The Shining Garment of the Text: Gendered Readings of John's Prologue* (JSNTSup 165; Gender, Culture, Theory 6; Sheffield: Sheffield Academic Press, 1998); Elisabeth Schüssler Fiorenza, *Jesus: Miriam's Child, Sophia's Prophet: Critical Issues in Feminist Christology* ([New York: Continuum, 1994], 152–54); and Elizabeth A. Johnson, *She Who Is: The Mystery of God in Feminist Theological Discourse* ([New York: Crossroad, 1994], 96–99).
2. Significant exceptions to that generalization have been the work of Scott mentioned above; studies by Elizabeth Harris (*Prologue and Gospel: The Theology of the Fourth Evangelist* [JSNTSup 107; Sheffield: Sheffield Academic Press, 1994]) and Michael E. Willett (*Wisdom Christology in the Fourth Gospel* [San Francisco: Mellen Research University Press, 1992]); and the commentary by Ben Witherington, III (*John's Wisdom: A Commentary on the Fourth Gospel* [Louisville, Ky.: Westminster John Knox Press, 1995]). Insights of these authors will be introduced throughout the discussion that follows.
3. Raymond E. Brown, *The Gospel according to John,* AB 29A (Garden City, N.Y.: Doubleday & Co., 1966), 3–4. For an alternative approach, see Jeff Staley, "The Structure of John's Prologue: Its Implications for the Gospel's Narrative Structure," *CBQ* 48 (1986): 241–63. Staley identifies a chiastic structure, as follows:

> A. vv. 1–5—the λόγος and God
>
> > B. vv. 6–8—John the Baptist
> >
> > > C. vv. 9–11—the λόγος and light
> > >
> > > > D. vv. 12–13—power to become children of God
> > >
> > > C'. v. 14—the λόγος becomes flesh
> >
> > B'. v. 15—John the Baptist
>
> A'. vv. 16–18—the λόγος and humankind

Michael Willett (*Wisdom Christology,* 31–34) recognizes three sections of the poem: vv. 1–5—the word in the beginning; vv. 9–13—the word in the world; and vv. 14, 16–18—the word in the community.

4. See Adele Reinhartz, *The Word in the World: The Cosmological Tale in the Fourth Gospel* (SBLMS 45; Atlanta: Scholars Press, 1992).
5. R. Alan Culpepper, "The Gospel of John as a Document of Faith in a Pluralistic Culture," in *"What Is John?" Readers and Readings in the Fourth Gospel* (SBL Symposium Series 3; ed. Fernando F. Segovia; Atlanta: Scholars Press, 1996), 107–27.
6. The case has frequently been made that other christological hymns known in the early church (such as Phil. 2:6–11 and Col. 1:15–20) also have their roots in hymns about divine Wisdom. These traces of those traditions used to proclaim the man from Nazareth who mediated life and wholeness to those communities, who died and yet lived, who was in the very particularity of his earthly presence also God-with-Us leads one to wonder whether the Sophia traditions may have played an important role in the piety and worship of at least some parts of Hellenistic Judaism.
7. Hans Weder, *"Deus Incarnatus:* On the Hermeneutics of Christology in the Johannine Writings," in *Exploring the Gospel of John: In Honor of D. Moody Smith* (ed. R. Alan Culpepper and C. Clifton Black; Louisville, Ky.: Westminster John Knox, 1996), 327–45.
8. José Porfirio Miranda, *Being and the Messiah: The Message of St. John* (Maryknoll, N.Y.: Orbis Books, 1977) 114–21.
9. I remain uncertain about how to understand the absence of the definite article in reference to God in this statement. To read it as "and the λόγος was a god"—implying one among a number of them, but presumably not to be equated with the "real" God whom they worshiped—is a perspective not echoed anywhere else in the Gospel. On the other hand, elsewhere in the Gospel the definite article is used for God (ὁ θεός). Given what the author will go on to affirm about Jesus as the λόγος incarnate, my conclusion is to understand the verse as "and the λόγος was God," and simply to puzzle about the absence of the article. See the discussion of this problem in Scott, *Sophia,* 97.
10. The problem of pronouns can be avoided in the first strophe by rendering οὗτος as "that one" or "the same (one)." It becomes critical, however, in the second strophe.
11. Scott, *Sophia,* 114.
12. The emphasis on the power of the "name" of God, coupled with the more than one hundred occurrences of the designation of God as πατήρ in this Gospel, has supported the assertion in popular piety and in formal doctrinal reflection alike that "Father" is that divine "name." It seems to me that such a conclusion is unwarranted for at least two reasons. First, to refer to "the name," be it of Jesus or of God, invokes the full presence and power of the one referred to, not to a magic formula whose effectiveness depends on its accuracy. It is God or Christ who does the things indicated. Second, I am not even convinced that πατήρ functions as a "name" in most of the occurrences in this Gospel. Where it occurs in the vocative case in the context of prayers (11:41; 12:27, 28; and six times in the great prayer of John 17), it does seem to parallel the use of ἄββα elsewhere in the New Testament. In approximately one-third of the remaining occurrences, Jesus is said to refer to God as "my father," which seems to invoke the intimacy of their relationship as "father" and "son." The rest—well over eighty—refer simply to ὁ πατήρ, "the father." They occur in discourses where the relationship between Jesus and God is not a specific issue. In fact, one might even ask whether that term should be seen as a name for God or as a circumlocution for God, similar in function to the Matthean use of "reign of heaven" where Mark and Luke have "reign of God."
13. Scott, *Sophia,* 105.
14. Willett, *Wisdom Christology,* 43.
15. Early Christian usage favored χάρις to render the content of the Hebrew term חסד, even though the LXX usually used ἔλεος.
16. John 1:16 portrays that bounty in two ways. First, the word πλήρωμα points to a totality or completeness. Nothing is lacking. Second, the phrase χάρις ἀντὶ χάριτος could have a cumulative sense ("grace upon grace") instead of the meaning of re-

placement ("[this new?] grace instead of [the former?] grace"), as it is often translated. See the discussions in BAGD, 73–74; and Warren Carter, "The Prologue and John's Gospel: Function, Symbol and the Definitive Word," *JSNT* 39 (1990): 40.

17. Even that occurrence of πατήρ should perhaps be rendered as "parent" rather than "father," given the practice of using the masculine term when the biological gender of the actual referent is unspecified.

18. Willett, *Wisdom Christology,* 41.

19. This is the conclusion drawn by Martinus C. de Boer in *Johannine Perspectives on the Death of Jesus* (Kampen: Kok Pharos, 1996), 114. The underlying question, namely, whether the Fourth Gospel presents an "anti-Moses" perspective, will have to be examined through references to Moses elsewhere in the Gospel. That will be done in the second section of this chapter. In any event, any such conclusion should be held in abeyance on the basis of the evidence of this verse alone.

20. Oscar Cullmann ("The Theological Content of the Prologue to John in Its Present Form," in *The Conversation Continues: Studies in Paul and John* [ed. Robert T. Fortna and Beverly R. Gaventa; Nashville: Abingdon Press, 1990], 297–98) calls Jesus "the true 'exegete' of the divine being."

21. Recall again the debate over whether in Prov. 8:22 Wisdom is said to have been created by God or to have come to be in some other way. (See chapter 3, n. 19, above.)

22. Of the variety of readings of this verse found in ancient manuscripts, this one followed by *UBSGNT* 5 (with a "B" rating, indicating considerable confidence in their decision) is most persuasive, both on the basis of strong external evidence and on the basis of its being a more difficult reading than alternatives that insert the word "son" or present "God" in the genitive case.

23. I was working on this idea when I came upon the article "Logos Ecclesiology in John's Gospel," by Paul S. Minear (in *Christological Perspectives: Essays in Honor of Harvey K. McArthur* [ed. Robert F. Berkey and Sarah A. Edwards; New York: Pilgrim Press, 1982], 95–111). It is no longer clear to me which of the following points were mine before I found them in his article and which I owe solely to him. For that reason I will allow his article to shape this portion of the discussion.

24. Ibid., 100.

25. Ibid., 97–106.

26. Ibid., 106.

27. This dimension of the continuing intimacy between Jesus and God is expressed in the concluding commentary of 1:18 as well as in the first strophe of the hymn.

28. On this point, 12:35 echoes 1:5 in affirming that darkness has not been able to "overcome" (καταλαμβάνω) this light.

29. Catherine Cory, "Wisdom's Rescue: A New Reading of the Tabernacles Discourse (John 7:1–8:59," *JBL* 116 (1997): 95–116.

30. The notable exception, of course, is the selective use of the law attributed to Jesus' adversaries in the passion narrative (19:7).

31. Schüssler Fiorenza, *Jesus: Miriam's Child, Sophia's Prophet,* 152–54.

32. Among others, Luise Schottroff draws this conclusion about the portrait of Jesus as the provider of bread (*Lydia's Impatient Sisters: A Feminist Social History of Early Christianity* [Louisville, Ky.: Westminster John Knox Press, 1995], 85).

33. This pattern is evidenced in virtually every expression of the Sophia-myth. See the discussions in William O. Walker, Jr., "John 1.43–51 and 'The Son of Man' in the Fourth Gospel," *JSNT* 56 (1994): 31–42; and Wayne A. Meeks, "The Man from Heaven in Johannine Sectarianism," *JBL* 91: (1972) 44–72.

34. Even the pericope about the woman taken in adultery (omitted from many ancient manuscripts and perhaps not even originally a part of this Gospel) follows this pattern, as it is set in the temple square where he is teaching (7:53–8:11).

35. Note the explicit reference to his teaching in παροιμίαι in 10:15 and 16:25 (where he promises that in the hour that is coming, he will no longer use such figures).

36. See the discussion in Frédéric Manns, "La Sagesse Nouricière de l'Évangile de Jean," *Bibbia e Oriente* 194 (1997): 207–34.
37. Gary Burge, *The Anointed Community: The Holy Spirit in the Johannine Tradition* (Grand Rapids: Wm. B. Eerdmans Publishing Co., 1987), 102–3.
38. Jerome Neyrey, *An Ideology of Revolt: John's Christology in Social Science Perspective* (Philadelphia: Fortress Press, 1988), 214.
39. Ibid., 213; Elizabeth Harris, *Prologue and Gospel: The Theology of the Fourth Evangelist* (JSNTSup 107; Sheffield: Sheffield Academic Press, 1994), 130.
40. Harris, *Prologue and Gospel,* 137. See the argument of Sallie McFague that metaphor is the only appropriate vehicle for identifying God (*Metaphorical Theology: Models of God in Religious Language* [Philadelphia: Fortress Press, 1982] and *Models of God: Theology for an Ecological, Nuclear Age* [Philadelphia: Fortress Press, 1987], 29–57).
41. As Raymond Brown notes (*The Gospel according to John* [AB 29A; Garden City, N.Y.: Doubleday & Co., 1970], 666), one cannot ignore the connections between the themes of bread and the vine and the eucharistic imagery of the church, which can be seen even in the interpretation of the former in John 6:25–59. Brown notes further that it would be a mistake to attribute a note of polemic to the language of the "true vine" (in contrast to a presumed "false vine"). Rather, he suggests a connection to the "real vine" of the LXX of Jer. 2:21, where it is emphasized as the source of life (Ibid., 674–75).
42. The figure of the "good shepherd" may trace its roots to such traditions as the parable of the lost sheep that is attributed to Jesus in Matt. 18:12–14 and Luke 15:3–6 (Q).
43. The "way" in all of these examples, and in such occurrences in the literature of the Qumran community as 1QS ix 17–18 and CD i 3, is more properly seen as revelatory than simply moral language (though if the two can be distinguished, they cannot be separated), in that it identifies the avenue of salvation, as it does also in the Fourth Gospel.
44. Scott, *Sophia,* 172.
45. Brown, *John,* AB 29A, cxxiv.
46. Johnson, *She Who Is,* 99.
47. Schottroff, *Lydia's Impatient Sisters,* 85; Schüssler Fiorenza, *Jesus: Miriam's Child, Sophia's Prophet,* 152–54; Judith E. McKinley, *Gendering Wisdom the Host: Biblical Invitations to Eat and Drink* (*JSOT* 216; Gender, Culture, Theory 4; Sheffield: Sheffield Academic Press, 1996), 181.

CHAPTER 5: APPOINTED TO BE FRIENDS

1. Two recent studies examine aspects of this theme in the thought of the Gospel writer. The dissertation of Eldo Puthenkandathil (*Philos: A Designation for the Jesus-Disciple Relationship: An Exegetico-Theological Investigation of the Term in the Fourth Gospel* [Frankfurt: Peter Lang, 1993]) looks at friendship as a term that identifies the relationship of responsibility and revelation between Jesus and the disciples. A christological study by Josephine Massyngbaerde Ford (*Redeemer, Friend, and Mother: Salvation in Antiquity and in the Gospel of John* [Minneapolis: Fortress, 1997]) examines Wisdom's role as redeemer, friend, and mother according to various documents of antiquity, including the Fourth Gospel.
2. It is not clear whether the Johannine community would have been familiar with the metaphor of the church as the "bride of Christ." Recognizing the reference to wedding roles in popular culture is probably the best interpretive key by which to understand the term here, i.e., as a way to identify the relative importance of Jesus and John.
3. Ben Witherington, III, *John's Wisdom: A Commentary on the Fourth Gospel* (Louisville, Ky.: Westminster John Knox Press, 1995) 293–94; Bruce Malina and Richard Rohrbaugh, *Social Science Commentary on the Gospel of John* (Minneapolis: Fortress Press, 1998), 267; Raymond E. Brown, *The Gospel according to John* (AB 29A; Garden City, N.Y.: Doubleday & Co., 1970), 893–95.

4. Fernando F. Segovia, *Love Relationships in the Johannine Tradition: Agape/Agapan in 1 John and the Fourth Gospel* (SBLDS 56; Chico, Calif.: Scholars Press, 1982), 134; Victor P. Furnish, *The Love Commandment in the New Testament* (Nashville: Abingdon Press, 1972), 134.

5. Brown, *John,* AB 29A, 598–600, 611; Furnish, *Love Commandment,* 134–35.

6. Fernando F. Segovia, *The Farewell of the Word: The Johannine Call to Abide* (Minneapolis: Fortress Press, 1991), 284–87.

7. R. Alan Culpepper, "The Johannine *Hypodeigma:* A Reading of John 13:1–38," *Semeia* 53 (1991): 133–52.

8. Brown, *John,* AB 29A, 667.

9. It is important to note that the verb τίθημι, which is usually translated as "lay down" (one's life) in 15:13, is the same one translated as "appoint" in v. 16. Clearly the assumption that v. 13 refers to Jesus' approaching death as his ultimate salvific act "for his friends" has influenced translators in these different renderings of the same verb in this passage. Translating both occurrences by the same English verb "appoint," however, changes the emphasis of the first from death as itself the *purpose,* to death as the *consequence* of the intended "appointment" or engagement of Jesus' life. A similar shift in meaning can be seen in 1 John 3:16 when τίθημι is translated as "appoint" rather than as "lay down."

10. Martin Dibelius, "Joh 15,13: Eine Studie zum Traditionsproblem des Johannes-Evangeliums," *Botschaft und Geschichte* (2 vols.; Tübingen: J. C. B. Mohr, 1953), 1:204–20.

11. It is impossible to know for certain whether this conjunction of Christology and ethics began with the author of the Gospel or whether he found the link already in the sources on which he drew. (See Fernando F. Segovia, "The Theology and Provenance of John 15:1–17," *JBL* 101 [1982]: 115–28.) Two factors lead me to think that the connection had already been made in the theological formulations of his community, whether or not it took written form in his sources. The first is the way their integration is built into the literary structure of sections of the Gospel (like chap. 15). The second is the non-polemical rhetoric by which the connection is drawn, as if the author needed only to recall and not to persuade.

12. See *Mandaean Literature,* 79, 108, 139, 193, 205.

13. Brown, *John,* AB 29A, 682–83; R. Schnackenburg, *The Gospel according to St. John* (3 vols.; New York: Crossroad, 1982), 3:109–10; Rudolf Bultmann, *The Gospel of John: A Commentary* (Philadelphia: Westminster Press, 1971), 544–45 n. 7.

14. Ernst Käsemann, *The Testament of Jesus: A Study of the Gospel of John in the Light of Chapter 17* (Philadelphia: Fortress Press, 1968), 31.

15. The following list represents only a few of the scholars who draw this conclusion: Werner Kelber, "Metaphysics and Marginality in John," in *"What Is John?" Readers and Readings of the Fourth Gospel* (SBL Symposium Series 3; ed. Fernando F. Segovia; Atlanta: Scholars Press, 1996), 129–54; Raymond F. Collins, *These Things Have Been Written: Studies on the Fourth Gospel* (Grand Rapids: Wm. B. Eerdmans Publishing Co., 1990), 217; David K. Rensberger, *Johannine Faith and Liberating Community* (Philadelphia: Westminster Press, 1988), 79–80; Wolfgang Schrage, *The Ethics of the New Testament* (Philadelphia: Fortress Press, 1988), 316–19.

16. Segovia, *The Farewell of the Word,* 301–02.

17. Craig R. Koester, *Symbolism in the Fourth Gospel: Meaning, Mystery, Community* (Minneapolis: Fortress Press, 1995), 240–41.

18. Two collections of essays, both edited by John T. Fitzgerald, provide an overview of perspectives on friendship in the Hellenistic world in which the Fourth Gospel took shape. They are: *Greco-Roman Perspectives on Friendship* (SBL RBS 34; Atlanta: Scholars Press, 1997) and *Friendship, Flattery, and Frankness of Speech: Studies on Friendship in the New Testament World* (NovTSup 82; New York, Leiden, and Köln: E. J. Brill, 1996).

19. Gustav Stählin, "φιλέω, κτλ.," *TDNT,* 9:147–50.

20. Ronald F. Hock, "An Extraordinary Friend in Chariton's *Callirhoe:* The Importance of Friendship in the Greek Romances," in Fitzgerald, ed., *Greco-Roman Perspectives on Friendship,* 145–62.

21. It should be noted that Lucian scorns the examples of loyalty and risk-taking found in the romantic novels of his day as unworthy of the label "friendship." See the discussion in Richard I. Pervo, "With Lucian: Who Needs Friends? Friendship in the *Toxaris,*" in Fitzgerald, ed., *Greco-Roman Perspectives on Friendship,* 163–80.

22. Stählin, φιλέω, 154–56.

23. In both Isa. 41:8 and 2 Chron. 20:7, the Hebrew word translated into English as "friend" is אֹהֵב, "beloved" or "loved one."

24. Exodus 33:11 compares the manner of God's speech to Moses to the way one friend speaks to another, but the analogy is adverbial. The text stops short of calling Moses God's friend.

25. Kathleen M. O'Connor, *The Wisdom Literature* (Wilmington, Del.: Michael Glazier, 1988) 156–57. Consistent with the intended audience of this book, however, women and slaves were not included in such affirmations.

26. There are several references of a proverbial sort to friendship in such Talmudic passages as *Baba Batra* I and *Berakot* IX, but due to the difficulty of dating these texts with any certainty, it seemed best not to consider them in sketching the context out of which the Fourth Gospel emerged.

27. Bruce C. Birch, *1 and 2 Samuel* (NIB; Nashville: Abingdon Press, 1998), 2:1133.

28. Ibid., 1133; Katharine Doob Sakenfeld, *Faithfulness in Action: Loyalty in Biblical Perspective* (Philadelphia: Fortress Press, 1985), 1–15.

29. Katharine Doob Sakenfeld, *The Meaning of Hesed in the Hebrew Bible: A New Inquiry* (HSM 17; Missoula, Mont.: Scholars Press, 1978), 233–34.

30. Phyllis Trible, *God and the Rhetoric of Sexuality* (OBT; Philadelphia: Fortress, 1978), 169–70.

31. Following the exile, when the public institutions of Israel's life were being rebuilt, the household—the private space where women lived and worked—was the primary social and economic unit. Thus, despite public laws still oriented toward patriarchal dominance in the society, in practice women often exercised considerable influence and even power. See the discussion in Carol Meyers, "Returning Home: Ruth 1.8 and the Gendering of the Book of Ruth," *Feminist Companion to Ruth* (ed. Athalya Brenner; Sheffield: Sheffield Academic Press, 1993), 111.

32. Concerning the postexilic dating of Ruth, see André Lacocque, *The Feminine Unconventional: Four Subversive Figures in Israel's Tradition* (OBT; Minneapolis: Fortress Press, 1990), 91–92; Renate Jost, *Freundin in der Fremde: Rut und Noemi* (Stuttgart: Quell Verlag, 1992), 8–9.

33. See the discussions in Fokkelien Van Dijk-Hemmes, "Ruth: A Product of Women's Culture?" (134–39) and Athalya Brenner, "Naomi and Ruth" (70–84) and "Naomi and Ruth: Further Reflections" (140–44), all in *Feminist Companion to Ruth;* and Richard Bauckham, "The Book of Ruth and the Possibility of a Feminist Canonical Hermeneutic," *Biblical Interpretation* 5 (1997): 29–45.

34. Ilana Pardes, *Countertraditions in the Bible: A Feminist Approach* (Cambridge: Harvard University Press, 1992), 111.

35. Lacocque, *Feminine Unconventional,* 115–16; BDB, 924, 946.

36. Jost, *Freundin in der Fremde,* 74; Mieke Bal, "Heroism and Proper Names, or the Fruits of Analogy," in *Feminist Companion to Ruth,* 63–64.

37. See the discussion of the role of female characters in the Fourth Gospel in Martin Scott, *Sophia and the Johannine Jesus* (JSNTSup 71; Sheffield: Sheffield Academic Press, 1992) 174–240; and Raymond E. Brown, *The Community of the Beloved Disciple: The Life, Loves, and Hates of an Individual Church in New Testament Times* (New York: Paulist Press, 1979), 183–98.

38. That affirmation concerning Jesus' role also echoes the view of God as *goʻel* of Israel seen in Isa. 41:14, which follows the reference in Isa. 41:8 to Abraham as "friend of God." The juxtaposition of the images of "redeemer" and "friend" occurs, then, in three different texts emerging from communities shaped by the experience of exile or diaspora. An additional link between the figure of the *goʻel* in Ruth and the Fourth Gospel is the possible link of that role to the παράκλητος, as suggested by Lacocque's reading of the Hebrew term as "counselor" (*Feminine Unconventional,* 94). That meaning is marginal to the general use of the term, and certainly to the term in the story of Ruth, and should probably not be imported into the discussion of the term παράκλητος in chapter 6 of this study.

39. Of 118 occurrences of the word in the New Testament, forty are in the Fourth Gospel and twenty-seven in the Johannine epistles. See Gary M. Burge, *The Anointed Community: The Holy Spirit in the Johannine Tradition* (Grand Rapids: Wm. B. Eerdmans Publishing Co., 1987), 118.

40. Collins, *These Things Have Been Written,* 53.

41. Martin Scott, *Sophia and the Johannine Jesus* (JSNTSup 71; Sheffield: Sheffield Academic Press, 1992), 158.

42. Ibid., 157.

43. Käsemann, *Testament of Jesus,* 46.

44. This meaning of σημεῖον as an event that points to—and moves the narrative toward—the cross seems self-evident from the reference in John 3:14 to Num. 21:9, where the LXX uses that word for the "pole" on which the bronze serpent is lifted up, so that the people who see it will not die from the bite of the venomous serpents. In the context in John 3, the implication is that Nicodemus (and other "teachers of Israel") ought to understand that reference to Jesus' salvific role when he has been "lifted up" on the "pole" (that is, the cross).

45. Malina and Rohrbaugh, *Social Science Commentary on the Gospel of John,* 70–71.

46. Brown, *John,* AB 29A, 922–23.

47. How to translate καλός is not clear. "Model shepherd" may be preferable to the traditional "good shepherd." The same word used to describe the wine in 2:10 might well be rendered "choice" or "best"—clearly not a moral assessment, but one that relates to conformity to a norm or standard.

48. That image is supported by a romanticizing of Psalm 23 that does not take into account the ambivalence of the shepherd image elsewhere in the Hebrew Bible. (See, for example, Num. 27:16–17; Micah 2:12–13; 1 Kings 22:17; Jer. 10:21; 23:1–2; and Ezekiel 34. Witherington (*John's Wisdom,* 187) points to the setting of this narrative at the feast of Dedication, when Jews celebrate the military victory of the Maccabees and the recovery of the Holy City, a struggle in which some Maccabees had indeed lost their lives on behalf of the people. He suggests that for the Johannine community the παροιμία would have linked Jesus to that precious memory.

49. For a discussion of the connection between knowing a person's name and friendship, see Alan C. Mitchell, " 'Greet Friends by Name': NT Evidence for the Greco-Roman *Topos* on Friendship," in *Greco-Roman Perspectives on Friendship,* 225–62.

50. Malina and Rohrbaugh, *Social Science Commentary on the Gospel of John,* 182–83.

51. Brown, *John,* AB 29A, 387.

52. The statement of Peter in 13:37 and Jesus' reply in 13:38 also address Peter's willingness to risk his life—not an intention to seek death.

53. The connection between these two texts has been recognized by most interpreters. See, for example, the discussion in Brown, *John,* AB 29A, 1009–11; and Sandra M. Schneiders, "John 20:11–18: The Encounter of the Easter Jesus with Mary Magdalene—A Transformative Feminist Reading," in *"What Is John?,"* 163.

54. Schneiders, "John 20:11–18," 159.

55. The parallelism of the three questions and the three denials appears to be an obvious literary device to link the two episodes. The two are symmetrical, but the scene in John

21 does not undo the denials, for there is no hint, even at the end, that Peter understands the point at issue. It is the unrehabilitated Peter who gets the commission to tend the flock. (See Brown, *John,* AB 29A, 1110–11.) That too may be part of the author's commentary on the character of the Christian community.

56. As Brown points out (*John,* AB 29A, 1104) both imperatives, βόσκε and ποίμαινε, can translate the Hebrew word רעה.

CHAPTER 6: THE "OTHER PARACLETE": THE STORY CONTINUES

1. Thus, Raymond Brown identifies the παράκλητος as "the Spirit understood as the presence of the absent Jesus," who takes the place on earth of the glorified Jesus. See Raymond E. Brown, *The Gospel according to John,* (AB 29A; Garden City, N.Y.: Doubleday & Co., 1970), 710–11.

2. In the LXX, for example, the verb is often used in that sense to render such Hebrew verbs as נחם (Gustav Stählin, "παρακαλέω," *TDNT* 5:776–77).

3. Johannes Behm, "παράκλητος," *TDNT,* 5:801.

4. Ibid.

5. A similar division between the understanding of the word as "Advocate" and "Comforter" is reflected in early Christian usage of the term and in its historico-religious background (Ibid., 805–12).

6. The overlapping chiastic patterns identified by Wes Howard-Brook demonstrate this aspect of Johannine structure (*Becoming Children of God: John's Gospel and Radical Discipleship,* Maryknoll, N.Y.: Orbis Books, 1994, passim). I began working on chiastic patterns in sections of this Gospel prior to reading his commentary, and, while the suggestions presented here derive from my own work, they have inevitably been influenced by his, in ways too subtle to distinguish.

7. Ben Witherington, III, *John's Wisdom: A Commentary on the Fourth Gospel* (Louisville, Ky.: Westminster John Knox Press, 1995), 251.

8. Howard-Brook, *Becoming Children of God,* 319. See the discussion of this issue in chapter 5 of this study.

9. Brown, *John,* AB 29A, 638–39. Brown notes, however, that some have proposed to read the words appositively ("another, a Paraclete") to avoid the suggestion that this figure and Jesus are in any sense to be equated.

10. The definite article is essential, as "the truth" for John is singular, just as there is only one messiah (Howard-Brook, *Becoming Children of God,* 321). The "Spirit of truth," which is another way the παράκλητος is identified in the Fourth Gospel (14:17; 15:26; 16:13), is a term found elsewhere in the New Testament only in the closely related 1 John (2:1; 4:6; 5:6).

11. See this list in Gary M. Burge, *The Anointed Community: The Holy Spirit in the Johannine Tradition* (Grand Rapids: Wm. B. Eerdmans Publishing Co., 1987), 141. See also Brown, *John,* AB 29A, 1140–41; and Witherington, *John's Wisdom,* 251.

12. Brown, *John,* AB 29A, 715, 1139; Rudolf Schnackenburg, *The Gospel according to St. John* (3 vols.; New York: Crossroad, 1987), 3:134, 144; Howard-Brook, *Becoming Children of God,* 251.

13. Witherington, *John's Wisdom,* 251.

14. At first glance, it might seem that in the Fourth Gospel the Paraclete parallels the role of the λόγος in Philo, which functions as a bridge-figure between the divine and human realms when that function is taken away from σοφία. The underlying argument is different, however. In the Fourth Gospel the fact that Wisdom—already called the λόγος—is incarnate in a physical human life (itself a notion that would be foreign to Philo) is what limits the time when that form of presence is possible. Chronology, and not gender-based philosophical arguments, accounts for the shift.

15. Heinrich Seesemann, "ὀρφανός," *TDNT,* 5:487–88. See also Howard-Brook, *Becoming Children of God,* 321.

16. As R. Alan Culpepper argues (*The Johannine School: An Examination of the Johannine-School Hypothesis Based on an Investigation of the Ancient Schools* [SBLDS 26; Missoula, Mont.: Scholars Press, 1975], 267–70; and *Anatomy of the Fourth Gospel: A Study in Literary Design* [Philadelphia: Fortress Press, 1983], 122–23), since it is the Beloved Disciple's role as "witness" to remind the others of Jesus' words and deeds, that disciple functions as the Paraclete is said to do in 14:26. However, to restrict the Paraclete to embodiment in that disciple (and perhaps to a sort of apostolic succession from him) seems to me inappropriately individualistic. The emphasis in this section of the discourse on mutuality of responsibility and on plural nouns and pronouns suggests rather a broader presence of the Paraclete in the community of believers.

17. The location of comfort and assurance as well as the responsibility of discipleship in the life of the community is conveyed grammatically by the second-person plural forms in vv. 15–20, which are joined seamlessly to third-person singular forms (e.g., "the one who . . . ") in v. 21.

18. See the discussion in Witherington, *John's Wisdom,* 251.

19. Brown, *John,* AB 29A, 1138. See also Schnackenburg, *St. John,* 3:146; Burge, *The Anointed Community,* 6.

20. It is interesting to note that in Qumran documents the angelic figure who would lead Israel's final battle against the prince of darkness is often called "the spirit of truth" (Howard-Brook, *Becoming Children of God,* 320, citing A. R. C. Leaney, in *John and the Dead Sea Scrolls* [ed. James H. Charlesworth; New York: Crossroad, 1990], 43–44).

21. On this point, I disagree with D. A. Carson ("The Function of the Paraclete in John 16:7–11," *JBL* 98 [1979]: 547–66), who dismisses the role of the particles and concludes that in all three cases the ὅτι tells why the Paraclete has the particular task.

CHAPTER 7: CONCLUSIONS AND IMPLICATIONS

1. Roberto S. Goizueta, *Caminemos con Jesús: Toward a Hispanic/Latino Theology of Accompaniment* (Maryknoll, N.Y.: Orbis Books, 1995), 9.

2. Ibid., 194, quoting Juan Carlos Scannone, "Un nuevo punto de partida en la filosofía latinoamericana," *Stromata* 36 (1980): 32.

Index of Scripture and Other Ancient Literature